1,000,000 Books

are available to read at

www.ForgottenBooks.com

Read online
Download PDF
Purchase in print

ISBN 978-1-330-62177-6
PIBN 10083630

This book is a reproduction of an important historical work. Forgotten Books uses state-of-the-art technology to digitally reconstruct the work, preserving the original format whilst repairing imperfections present in the aged copy. In rare cases, an imperfection in the original, such as a blemish or missing page, may be replicated in our edition. We do, however, repair the vast majority of imperfections successfully; any imperfections that remain are intentionally left to preserve the state of such historical works.

Forgotten Books is a registered trademark of FB &c Ltd.
Copyright © 2018 FB &c Ltd.
FB &c Ltd, Dalton House, 60 Windsor Avenue, London, SW19 2RR.
Company number 08720141. Registered in England and Wales.

For support please visit www.forgottenbooks.com

1 MONTH OF FREE READING

at
www.ForgottenBooks.com

By purchasing this book you are eligible for one month membership to ForgottenBooks.com, giving you unlimited access to our entire collection of over 1,000,000 titles via our web site and mobile apps.

To claim your free month visit:
www.forgottenbooks.com/free83630

* Offer is valid for 45 days from date of purchase. Terms and conditions apply.

English
Français
Deutsche
Italiano
Español
Português

www.forgottenbooks.com

Mythology Photography **Fiction**
Fishing Christianity **Art** Cooking
Essays Buddhism Freemasonry
Medicine **Biology** Music **Ancient Egypt** Evolution Carpentry Physics
Dance Geology **Mathematics** Fitness
Shakespeare **Folklore** Yoga Marketing
Confidence Immortality Biographies
Poetry **Psychology** Witchcraft
Electronics Chemistry History **Law**
Accounting **Philosophy** Anthropology
Alchemy Drama Quantum Mechanics
Atheism Sexual Health **Ancient History**
Entrepreneurship Languages Sport
Paleontology Needlework Islam
Metaphysics Investment Archaeology
Parenting Statistics Criminology
Motivational

THE DOMINION OF DREAMS

BY THE SAME AUTHOR

Pharais: A Romance of the Isles.

The Mountain Lovers: A Romance.

The Sin-Eater, and other Tales.

The Washer of the Ford, and other Tales.

Reissue Shorter Tales, with Others:—
>   I. Spiritual Tales.
>   II. Barbaric Tales.
>   III. Tragic Romances.

The Laughter of Peterkin: Old Celtic Tales Retold.

From the Hills of Dream: Poems.

IN PREPARATION

A Jacobite Romance.

The Reddening of the West: Studies in the Spiritual History of the Gael.

THE DOMINION
OF DREAMS

BY

FIONA MACLEOD

'L'homme a voulu rêver, le rêve gouvernera l'homme'
LE THÉÂTRE DE SÉRAPHIN

WESTMINSTER
ARCHIBALD CONSTABLE AND CO.
2 WHITEHALL GARDENS, S.W.
1899

*. . . . . . . For I have seen
In lonely places, and in lonelier hours,
My vision of the rainbow-aureoled face
Of her whom men name Beauty: proud, austere:
Dim vision of the far immortal Face,
Divinely fugitive, that haunts the world,
And lifts man's spiral thought to lovelier dreams.*

TO

EILIDH

THIS BOOK OF DREAMS

THAT ARE REALITIES

'Les choses de la terre n'existent que bien peu, et la vraie réalité n'est que dans les rêves.'
Les Paradis Artificiels.

'The song is the bird's self: and the song and its inspiration are one. . . . A bird flies past me, out of the west: I ask the fugitive, Is it with my love as of yore? I ask, in turn, the drifting cloud, the wind. . . . You ask of me a song: of me, who am but the lyre. Ask it of Love, my dear one: it is he who is the poet.'
From the Magyar.

'Who is it, therefore, that will speak of the visible such as it is? He who sees it.'
PLOTÎNUS.

'Le monde est grand: plus grand que le monde est le rêve:
Le ciel est vaste: plus vaste que le ciel est le désir.'
A. LE BRAZ.

THE FOUR WINDS OF THE SPIRIT

CONTENTS

DALUA
BY THE YELLOW MOONROCK
~~THE HOUSE OF SAND AND FOAM~~
LOST
THE WHITE HERON
CHILDREN OF THE DARK STAR
ALASDAIR THE PROUD
THE AMADAN
THE HERDSMAN

II

THE BOOK OF THE OPAL
THE WELLS OF PEACE
IN THE SHADOW OF THE HILLS
THE DISTANT COUNTRY
A MEMORY OF BEAUTY

III

THE SAD QUEEN
THE WOMAN WITH THE NET
ENYA OF THE DARK EYES

viii THE DOMINION OF DREAMS

	PAGE
HONEY OF THE WILD BEES	247
THE BIRDS OF EMAR	260
ULAD OF THE DREAMS	275
THE CRYING OF WIND	314

EPILOGUE

THE WIND, THE SHADOW, AND THE SOUL . .	323
(Bibliographical Note)	328

I

A

'*I have seen all things pass and all men go
Under the shadow of the drifting leaf.*'
                    (The Hour.)

'. . . *Only to gods in heaven
Comes no old age or death of anything;
All else is turmoiled by our master Time.
The earth's strength fades and manhood's glory fades,
Faith dies, and unfaith blossoms like a flower.
And who shall find in the open streets of men,
Or secret places of his own heart's love,
One wind blow true for ever.* . . .'
                    SOPHOCLES: Œdipus at Colônus.

'*A dream about a shadow is man: yet when
some God-given splendour falls, a glory of light
comes over him, and his life is sweet.*'
                    PINDAR.

DALUA

I have heard you calling, Dalua,
  Dalua !
I have heard you on the hill,
By the pool-side still,
Where the lapwings shrill
  Dalua . . . Dalua . . . Dalua !

What is it you call, Dalua,
  Dalua !
When the rains fall,
When the mists crawl,
And the curlews call
  Dalua . . . Dalua . . . Dalua !

I am the Fool, Dalua,
  Dalua !
When men hear me, their eyes
Darken: the shadow in the skies
Droops: and the keening-woman cries
  Dalua . . . Dalua . . . Dalua !

ONE night when Dan Macara was going over the hillside of Ben Breacan, he saw a tall man playing the pipes, and before him a great flock of sheep.

It was a night of the falling mist that makes a thin soundless rain. But behind the blurr was a rainpool of light, a pool that oozed into a wan flood; and so Macara knew that the moon was up,

---

* Dalua, one of the names of a mysterious being in the Celtic mythology, the Fairy Fool.

[handwritten: Amadan-Dhu, The Dark Witless One, or]

and was riding against the drift, and would pull the rain away from the hill.

Even in rain, with damp moss or soaking heather, sheep do not go silently. Macara wondered if they were all young rams, that there was not a crying *uan* or a bleating ewe to be heard. 'By the Black Stone of Iona,' he muttered, 'there is not even a broken *oisg* among them.'

True, there was a faint rising and falling *méh-ing* upper darkness of the hillside; but that sound, was confused with the rustling of many leaves of ash and birch, with eddies of air through the heather and among the fronds of the bracken, and with the perplexed uncertain hum of trickling waters. No one utterance slid cleanly through the gloom, but only the voice of darkness as it speaks among the rainy hills.

As he stumbled along the path, stony and rain-gutted, but held together by the tough heather-fibres, he thought of the comfortable room he had left in the farmhouse of Padruic and Mary Macrae, where the shadows were as warm as the peat-flames, and the hot milk and whisky had been so comfortable too; and warm and comfortable both, the good friendly words of Padruic and Mary.

He wiped the rain from his wet lips, and smiled as he remembered Mary's words: 'You, now, so tall and big, an' not ill-looking at that, for a dark Macara . . . and yet with no woman to your side! . . . an' you with the thirty years on you! . . . for sure I would have shame in going through the Strath, with the girls knowing that!' But just then he heard the broken notes of the feadan, or 'chanter,' that came from the tall man playing the pipes, with the great flock of sheep before him. It was like the flight of pee-wits, all this way and that.

'What with the dark and the rain and the whisky and the good words of Mairi Bàn, my head's like a black bog,' he muttered; 'and the playing of that man there is like the way o' voices in the bog.'

Then he heard without the ~~bog-cotton~~ in his ears. The air came faint but clear. It angered him. It was like a mocking voice. Perhaps this was because it was like a mocking voice. Perhaps because it was the old pipe-song, 'Oighean bhoidheach, slan leibh!' 'Ye pretty maids, farewell!' 'Who will he be?' he wondered sullenly. 'If it's Peter Macandrew, Ardmore's shepherd, I'll play him a tune behind the wind that he won't like.'

Then the tall man suddenly changed his chanter-music, and the wet night was full of a wild, forlorn, beautiful air.

Dan Macara had never heard that playing before, and he did not like it. Once, when he was a child, he had heard his mother tell Iain Dall, a blind piper of the Catanach, to stop an air that he was playing, because it had sobs and tears in it. He moved swiftly now to overtake the man with the flock of sheep. His playing was like Iain Dall's. He wanted, too, to ask him who he was, and whose chanter-magic he had, and where he was going (and the hill way at that!) with all those sheep.

But it took him a long time to get near. He ran at last, but he got no nearer. '*Gu ma h-olc dhut* . . . ill befall thee,' he cried angrily after a time; 'go your own way, and may the night swallow you and your flock.'

And with that, Dan Macara turned to follow the burnside-way again.

But once more the tall man with the flock of sheep changed the air that he was playing. Macara stopped and listened. It was sweet to hear. Was this a sudden magic that was played upon him? Had not the rain abruptly ceased, as a breath withdrawn? He stared confusedly: for sure, there was no rain, and moonlight lay upon the fern and upon a white birch that stood solitary in that white-green waste. The sprays of the birch were like a rain of pale shimmering gold. A bird slid along a topmost branch; blue, with breast like a white iris, and with wild-rose wings. Macara could see its eyes a-shine, two little starry flames. Song came from it, slow, broken, like water in a stony channel. With each note the years of Time ran laughing through ancient woods, and old age sighed across the world and sank into the earth, and the sea moaned with the burden of all moaning and all tears. The stars moved in a jocund measure; a player sat among them and played, the moon his footstool and the sun a flaming gem above his brows. The song was Youth.

Dan Macara stood. Dreams and visions ran past him, laughing, with starry eyes.

He closed his own eyes, trembling. When he opened them he saw no bird. The grey blurr of the rain came through the darkness. The cold green smell of the bog-myrtle filled the night.

But he was close to the shepherd now. Where had he heard that air? It was one of those old fonnsheen, for sure: yes, 'A Choillteach Ùrair,' 'The Green Woodland' . . . that was it. But he had never heard it played like that.

The man did not look round as Dan Macara drew near. The pipes were shadowy black, and had long black streamers from them. The man wore a Highland bonnet, with a black plume hanging from it.

The wet slurred moonshine came out as the rain ceased. Dan looked over the shoulder of the man at the long, straggling, crowd of sheep.

He saw then that they were only a flock of shadows.

They were of all shapes and sizes; and Macara knew, without knowing how he knew, that they were the shadows of all that the shepherd had found in his day's wandering—from the shadows of tall pines to the shadows of daisies, from the shadows of horned cattle to the shadows of fawns and field mice, from the shadow of a woman at a well to that of a wild rose trailing on the roadside, from the shadow of a dead man in a corrie, and of a boy playing on a reed with three holes, and the shadows of flying birds and drifting clouds, and the slow formless shadows of stones, to (as he saw with a sudden terror) the shadow of Dan Macara himself, idly decked with feather-like bracken, where he had lost it an hour ago in the darkness, when he had first heard the far-off broken lilt of the pipes.

Filled with an anger that was greater than his terror, Dan Macara ran forward, and strove to grasp the man by the shoulder; but with a crash he came against a great slab of granite, with its lichened sides wet and slippery with the hill-mist. As he fell, he struck his head and screamed. Before silence and darkness closed in upon him like two waves, he heard Dalua's mocking laughter far up among the hills, and saw a great flock of curlews rise from where the shadows had been.

When he woke there was no more mist on the hill. The moonlight turned the raindrops on the bracken into infinite little wells of light.

All night he wandered, looking for the curlew that was his shadow.

Towards the edge of day he lay down. Sleep was on him, soft and quiet as the breast-feather of a mothering bird. His head was in a tuft of grass: above it a star trailed a white flame — a silent solitude.

Dalua stood by him, brooding darkly. He was no shepherd now, but had trailing black hair like the thin shadows of branches at dusk, and wild eyes, obscure as the brown-black tarns in the heather.

He looked at the star, smiling darkly. Then it

moved against the dawn, and paled. It was no more. The man lay solitary.

It was the gloaming of the dawn. Many shadows stirred. Dalua lifted one. It was the shadow of a reed. He put it to his mouth and played upon it.

Above, in the greying waste, a bird wheeled this way and that. Then the curlew flew down, and stood quivering, with eyes wild as Dalua's. He looked at it, and played it into a shadow; and looked at the sleeping man, and played that shadow into his sleeping mind.

'There is your shadow for you,' he said, and touched Dan.

At that touch, Macara shivered all over. Then he woke with a laugh. He saw the dawn sliding along the tops of the pines on the east slope of Ben Breacan.

He rose. He threw his cromak away. Then he gave three wails of the wailing cry of the curlew, and wandered idly back by the way he had come.

It was years and years after that when I saw him.

'How did his madness come upon him?' I asked; for I recalled him strong and proud.

'The Dark Fool, the Amadan-Dhu, touched him. No one knows any more than that. But that is a true thing.'

He hated or feared nothing, save only shadows. These disquieted him, by the hearthside or upon the great lonely moors. He was quiet, and loved running water and the hill-wind. But, at times, the wailing of curlews threw him into a frenzy.

I asked him once why he was so sad. 'I have heard,' he said ... and then stared idly at me: adding suddenly, as though remembering words spoken by another:—'I have heard, the three lamentable elder voices of the world: the cry of the curlew on the hill, the wail of wind, and the sighing of the wave.'

He was ever witless, and loved wandering among the hills. No child feared him. He had a lost love in his face. At night, under the stars, his eyes showed stars as in a pool, but with a light more tender.

BY THE YELLOW MOONROCK

I

WHEN the word went through Strathraonull that the wife of Donald Macalister of Dalibrog had given birth to a child, there was rejoicing. Dalibrog himself was not so well pleased, for he had hoped that Morag his wife would ~~have borne~~ him a son; and as he was the most important man in the Strath, after the great Laird himself, he never doubted but that Morag would fulfil his trust in her. It was an ill thought, for him, that Seoras Macalister his brother ('an' him with such a starvin' big family behind him') should one day sit at Dalibrog, and care little whether or not the hill-rains were too heavy, whether some of the kye proved poor in milk, or if here or there a ewe or a lamb were lost. It was Seoras' way to care too little, or to say too little, about these things at the best of times; but if he were once at Dalibrog, out of that wet poor farm of his up in the hills, he would be glad every day of the days, and when he died the place would be worth less by a long way than it was now.

If only the lands of Dalibrog did not lie under entail, he could keep Seoras out. However, though

Morag had failed this time, she would do better next. 'It comes o' marrying a Mackenzie,' he muttered to himself at times; 'I never knew one of the breed yet that wouldn't be after doing just the very thing you wouldn't expect, and just because o' that same expecting.'

So he made the best of it when he learned that his firstborn was a girl.

The Strath folk cared nothing about his hopes or disappointment. Their rejoicing was because there were to be festivities at Dalibrog, and that every one from far and near was to be welcome. Donald Macalister had waited till he was forty before he married, and would not have changed his state then but that the fear of Seoras' big family was on him, for he loved Dalibrog better than kinship, or wife, or child.

The three great and as yet undivided and otherwise unfinished byres that had recently been added to the home farm—the model dairy it was already called, to the resentment of those whose dairies were painfully primitive—were to be filled with all who cared to come, and with meats and pastries and wine and beer and whisky enough to satisfy these, 'and as many more again.'

As the goings-on at Dalibrog fell on the popular day known throughout the Highlands as 'La Fheill Bride' (the Feast-day or Festival of St. Bride or Bridget), the stir was the greater. In every shepherd-sheiling and hill-bothie to the glen-crofts and the big farmhouses, preparation of some kind was made.

Among the good news which went from mouth to mouth, perhaps not the least welcome was that which told the coming of Rory M'Alpine the piper.

Every one knew Rory, and he was as welcome at each fireside along the Strath as he was at any hearth throughout the West, from the Cowal to the Torridons. There was no better piper than he, and, what was more, there was no one who had so great a store of old tales and new gossip; and he had a bad reputation, too, not for dishonesty, but for morals, though little evil against others was laid to him. 'Let Rory beware o' the whisky, and let the girls beware o' Rory,' had become a saying; with the result that the girls of the glens were over-curious, and that there was ever whisky and to spare for Piper Rory M'Alpine.

For more than a year, however, he had not set foot in the Strath. 'Strathraonull may whistle,' he said, 'but the curlew's on the hill'—by which he meant that the Strath folk might look in vain for him or his pipes or tales.

For on the Hallowe'en of the preceding year Rory had been enthusiastic. That was all he would ever admit: 'I had a great enthusiasm on me.' There had been a big gathering at the manse of the Rev. Kenneth Maclellan to celebrate the marriage of his daughter Jessie to the son of Sir Hector MacInnes, a great laird over away from Strathraonull. Rory had played with all his genius (the words are his); he had told old tales, and invented others old and new, and had spread gossip with a splendid impartiality; and, in a word, from noon till sundown had proved beyond all doubt that Rory M'Alpine was quite the most important person present, after the bridegroom, and a good deal more entertaining. As for the bride, she meant well, but if she had not had a mighty big tocher she would never have got young Ewan MacInnes; so they said.

By sundown on that memorable day, however, Rory had become so puffed up with his own elation and the sound of continual laughing praise, that he had drunk at least thrice the great quantity he was accustomed to allow as his 'measure.' He said afterwards that the misfortune of that night came about through the meanness of the Reverend Kenneth, who had given him some whisky that Black Donald himself would have found a murthering poison; 'for no gentleman,' he added, 'would get drunk all at once on good whisky,' forgetting, no doubt, that six hours' preliminary appreciation was a fair allowance. Whatever the reason was, he lost his good sense and good manners, and while the Reverend Kenneth was at prayer in the schoolhouse (that had been got up as a ballroom for the wedding-party), Rory's pipes were heard coming near and nearer, jigging a blasphemous, merry dance; and then, while every one was trying to look solemn, the door swung open, and Rory himself strutted in, playing an old, wicked wedding-pibroch that was a shame there in that place given over to prayer and thanksgiving. Some smiled, some laughed, but most frowned or shook their heads with shocked reproving glances. The minister was sore angry, and at last let go his pulpit voice and shouted to the piper to take himself off.

'An' for why that?' cried Rory, stopping to take breath, and cocking his head on one side, and winking hard this way and that, as though he were in a company of shepherds and drovers in a mountain-dew cabin.

'Because we are decent folk praising the Lord, an' we want none o' your rant, Rory M'Alpine!'

'Hoots, Mr. Maclellan, we're a' men an' women the night. It's no' every night that a quean is bedded wi' a——'

'That'll do, ye sumph,' shouted the minister angrily, 'an' get out o' this at once, for it's shameless drunk you are, you and your pipes too.'

But Rory only laughed at this. Then he threw back the pipes and tilted the chanter and let fly a long wailing screech; and in a minute or less the schoolhouse rang with the dancing, sweet, evil delight of 'The Hare amongst the Corn.' The tune was like a live thing, a leaping flame, and sprang this way and that, and laughed and screamed and jeered and mocked, and made men flush and stir, and the women grow white and nervous.

Suddenly two or three men, then half a dozen and more, put their arms round the waists of struggling, blushing girls; and a madness came upon every one there, and all kissed and hugged, and the younger ones swung to and fro in confused rough dance; while the minister, black in the face, thumped on the big Bible like Peter Mackechnie, the six-foot-four drummer down Fort William way, and Rory M'Alpine played an' played an' played till the veins stood out on his face, and his breath jerked like a jumping ewe at a gangway.

There is no saying what would have come of that tantarran (and evil enough came if all be true that's said, ' forbye the shame of it in that place an' at that hour an' before the Lord,' as Mr. Maclellan declared on the Sabbath that followed, when every one had bad headaches and stricken consciences) if Rory had not flung his pipes to the ground, and then danced on them with wild screeches and up-flung fists, and seized good Mistress Sarah, the minister's wife, and swung her this way and that in a touzled devil-may-care of a Highland reel, and had then kissed and hugged her with drunken amorous cries, and suddenly wept with loud hiccoughs and sobs, and then fallen like a wind-stricken scarecrow off its pole to lie in a shapeless, senseless heap at her feet.

Three elders and some young men carried Rory out, while Mr. Maclellan fanned his breathless, terrified wife with a hymn-book, and dried her scandalised tears with her new brown boa, and whispered blessed texts of Scripture and less holy words of marital exhortation.

The village-pond was not a score yards away, and they flung Rory into it, and John Macmillan the carpenter pitched the trampled broken pipes in after him; so that when, half sobered and panting for life, the piper struggled to his feet, and stood drenched and forlorn—'with all the enthusiasm out o' me,' as he said afterwards—he appeared dripping and dishevelled with a shapeless mass over his head and shoulders, and two great prongs like horns sticking out: 'for all the world like an awfu', beast in the Apocalypse,' related, later, one of the elders to an understanding and sympathetic audience, who had their own associations with apocalyptic visions of the kind.

And out of all that came not only a cruel, heavy cold for Rory, and the shame of a preaching against him on the Sabbath, but the black looks of every lad and lass who had been led to sin because of his lawless bad music, and of every douce man and woman who wondered if the neighbours had seen anything forbye the common on 'that awfu' night.' He had no money, and his pipes were wrecked, and couldn't give out even the poor drone of a hymn, or a 'Praise ye the Lord'; and he had his cruel cold on him, with hunger and a starving thirst.

He had slept that night at the warm side of a hayrick, but it was drizzly and drear chill when he woke at the greying. He looked sullenly at his drenched clothes and the tattered remnant of his pipes, and held the broken chanter in his hand, while he muttered black curses on those who lead innocent men into evil ways, and on drink in general, and whisky in particular, and, above all, on 'that water o' mildew out of an old ancient ink-bottle,' which Mr. Maclellan had given him; and cursed the minister, and all the folk in Strathraonull, with the coughing sickness to the cows and rot to the sheep, and a stake through the belly for that bitter misfit o' a man Macmillan who had ruined his pipes, and a black curse on the pipes themselves, and on the falling rain, and on the cold and hunger and bitter black thirst he had.

Then he sat down among the dry hay again, and tears ran down his face, because there was no pity in the world, and no God, and in his wet pockets never a pipeful of tobacco nor a match to light old cinders with for the whiff of a whiff.

He put his right hand to his breast to feel if his broken heart had still a beat to it, when his fingers touched something cold and hard. For a moment he dreamed God's mercy had left him a forgotten pipe, but the next he recognised a tin whistle he had bought three weeks before at a booth Glenshiel way, and had played on often since. He was in little mood for tin whistles or any other clamjaffry after what the pipes had led him to, but mechanically he began to blow a few dismal notes. Then an air came into the whistle and sang itself. It was like wild bees coming out of the heather, when the notes crept humming or singing or laughing out of the holes in the tin tube. Rory wondered what the air was. He played idly, and it came again. He knew it now; it was 'O'er the hills and far away.' While the drizzle soaked his stained rusty hair (red enough in the sunlight, or when he was talking and smiling before the peats, or playing reels in a barn to the flames of pine-torches), a shine came into his blue eyes. He played the sweet dreamy air three times. Then, with a sigh, he played a song he loved, ' A'' Chruinneag Ileach ' (The Islày Maid), and put the tin flute on his knee when he had ended, and stared before him, with the wet in his blue eyes, while words of the song fell from his lips :—

'Och, och mar tha mi ! 's mi nam aonar
. . . .
O sorrow upon me that I 'm here so lonely,
With black Despair with my heart in his grip :
There 's tears in my eyes for each drop from the skies,
And my love is gone from me like vows from the lip.'

Then he lifted the tin flute again, and played air upon air. And soon he forgot the heavy cold that was on him, and the chill and the empty belly and the bad thirst, and all the bitter evils of the world. He saw green glens waving in warm wind, and streams with fish splashing a whiteness over the running blue, and meadows filled with cattle gleaming white and red in the sunshine; or long fields of green corn or yellow wheat, lifting lances of flame under flying banners of the shadows of white clouds; or still lochs crimpled with the little dancing feet o' moonshine; or great lonely moors, with grey-brown ptarmigan fleeting from rock to rock, or a kestrel hawking like a drift of wind-blown rain, and nothing more to be seen or heard in all the waste but a woman with white shoulders and long black hair sitting by a tarn and singing a wild forlorn song, evil-sweet ; or he saw quiet places, under the stars, and an unknown folk moving blithely to and fro, and singing and laughing, all clad in green, like moonbeams in lily sheaths he thought. One of these delicate glad people came close to him, and played a little wild fantastic air, and Rory's tears fell because of his broken pipes, and because he could not capture the sighs and laughter of faëry, and he felt a sob in his heart when the slim green harper laughed, and he looked and could see nothing but a white foxglove in the moonshine, and heard nothing but a chime of little tinkling bells.

He came out of his dreams at that, and put a black curse on the slow-falling rain. Then, remembering the day it was, he played softly 'The Lord's my Shepherd,' and part of a hymn called 'Ye little lambs of Zion,' which he had picked up not long since, one day when lying half sober to leeward of a Methodist prayer-meeting.

An old woman, passing near, heard it, and her heart went out to the poor man.

'Well, well now, an' is that you, Rory M'Alpine?' she said, half kindly, half dubious, because of the drear broken man she saw and his sore plight.

'It is just me an' no other, Widow Sheen,' he answered sadly; 'for sure there's none but God to have pity on a poor man that was travelling hard to see his own kith an' kin afore he died, an' fell down by the way, an' a bad fit at that, with the good pipes smashed too, an' not any tobacco upon him whatever, an' a broken heart to lift along the way.'

Sheen Macgregor was a tender soul, and she knew nothing of what had happened the night before. She was too old and sad to go to the merry-making.

She was now on her way to the kirk, but she turned and led Rory back to her turf-thatched cottage that was only a butt and a ben. Soon he grew warm before the glowing peats, and was glad to be in the dry clothes that had belonged to old Gregor Macgregor, while his own steamed in the comfortable heat. It was a true word he said when he told Widow Sheen that he had never known porridge like her porridge, or tasted them so sweet and wholesome, and that the milk was like a young cow's at clover-time. For a time he was uneasy, with restless eyes; for he had caught sight of a black bottle on a shelf. But when Sheen had taken it down, and poured him out a good glass of smoky Glenlivet, he praised God aloud, and said with tears in his eyes that his own mother had never been more tender sweet with him.

He had but slight hopes of the good thing; but when the old woman went to the drawers-head and lifted a jar, and filled his pipe for him, his gladness was a gladness indeed. When he lifted a bit of red peat and put it to the bowl of his pipe, and had his mouth and nose filled with the heavy good smoke, there was not a curse left in his heart.

After a time Widow Sheen said she would go now, but he prayed her to give him home a little longer.

'I'm hungry to hear the hymns,' she said simply.

'For sure now, if that's all you'll be hungry for,'

pleaded Rory eagerly, 'I'll play you more hymns in an hour than you'll hear in a week'—and with that (and the more readily, because there were only ashes in the bowl now) he put down his pipe, and took his tin whistle, and played softly by the fire.

Widow Sheen sat and listened. It gave her peace and glad, holy thoughts. And if, after a time, Rory remembered no more hymns, and played old airs of love and sorrowful sweet songs of partings and regrets, the tired old woman did not know, or, knowing, showed no sign, but folded her withered hands on her lap, and closed her eyes, and dreamed old dreams.

After a time Rory saw she slept, so he rose and filled his pipe again. He had filled his pouch, too, when he remembered what he was doing, and put the tobacco back. Two hours passed. Then Widow Sheen waked and bade Rory stay and share her Sabbath stoup of leek broth with part of a neck of mutton in it—a luxury due to Miss Maclellan, who had sent the meat to the old woman, along with a packet of tea, to make up for her absence from the great doings.

That he did gladly, and all afternoon he told her stories. She cared little for any gossip save of Strathraonull, and all the decent gossip of the region was already known to her; but she loved old tales, and wild uncanny legends of kelpies and water-horses and sea-bulls, of fairy-lovers and solitary walkers in the night, of the green-clad cailleach on the hillside singing her fatal song as she milked the wild deer, of the bewitched thorns under which folk lay down to awake witless, of horns heard in the moonshine, and strange forlorn music in desolate places, and of what came of these and other omens and perversities. Rory had a good voice, too, and he sang old 'Gaelic songs; and when by chance he sang 'Mo nighean donn,' and she remembered when she had first heard it, when Gregor her lad wooed her at the summer-sheiling high on Ben Chreagan, her heart gave way, and she rose and kissed Rory.

Then she gave him tea, with as many scones and butter as he could eat, and filled his pouch and gave him a parting glass; and so he went out into the late day, sweet and fragrant now, with quiet light lying on stone and tree; and warming the shadows into broad leaves or fans of living dusk.

But for a year thereafter Rory M'Alpine would have nothing to do with Strathraonull. He made many a bitter satire upon it and its folk; and these sayings went round the straths and outlying countries, till the Strathraonull people wished that Mr. Maclellan had just forborne with the poor man, and him in his natural state too, seeing the day it was; or else that he had been drowned in the pool; or that Widow Sheen had left him in the wet open, where as likely as not he would have died of his chill and his broken pipes.

Rory prospered, however, and in Strathanndra it was allowed that the piper had reformed, and was on his way to end his days in peace. He was not known to be drunk save at the quarters, and there was no scandal except on Martinmas Day, when in the market-place at Fort William he hated the law and hurled his heavy pipes at the head of Sheriff Macdougall, and brought that great and bulky gentleman to the ground like a felled steer.

For a time after the Strathraonull sorrow he had acted as a drover, an old ploy; then Strathanndra himself had given him the post of second shepherd; and if one bad night he had not piped the sheep over a broken ledge into a quarry (it was the Lammas-quarter, and he was enthusiastic), he would have been shepherd still. Since then he had acted as Strathanndra blacksmith in place of Allan Colquhoun, who had broken his leg, and was only too glad to get Rory to take his place and act for him. And when at the New Year Colquhoun celebrated Hogmanay with too great joy, and was found head foremost in a miry boghole, Rory M'Alpine succeeded him as blacksmith, and Strathanndra widows and girls looked on him as a good man and true.

For some weeks Rory worked hard at his fine reputation. But when first the Established man, and then the Free Church man, and then the new-come U.P. man, called and exhorted him, and he had to subscribe to this and subscribe to that, and had made promises to attend each of the kirks, and even to qualify for a communicant, and was finally offered the U.P. precentorship, he became restive, and longed to be up in the hills, or moving from place to place with his pipes.

The change would have come soon or late, but it was the Strathraonull message that brought it near.

When first the word came that Strathraonull was stricken with remorse for what had happened when Rory had last honoured it, the piper snorted like an angry stot. Later, with a big slow wave of his hand, he remarked that it was news to him to learn Strathraonull was still in existence. 'I remember a poor place o' that name,' he said, 'but I thought it had died off, ~~or been bought by a Glasgow man for a~~ ~~boot factory~~, or had emigryated at two-pound-ten a head, an' no thanks when ye get there.'

A second embassy was rebuffed less bitterly. Rory was secretly overjoyed to hear that all Strathraonull was agreed on one point—that there was no piper in the Highlands to surpass Rory M'Alpine, and no teller of old tales to compare with him, and none so welcome of an evening. But he was obdurate. He sent word back that in Strathanndra the folk knew when they were well off, and that he could be a precentor when he liked, and an elder too for the matter o' that, and in any one o' the three kirks: then, fearing that this might go for laughter, and remembering that ill-day at Fort William at Martinmas, and the prejudice of the magistracy against him ever since, he added bitterly, 'A poor, poor place Strathraonull! Sure it has only one gentleman in it, an' that's a woman—old Widow Sheen Macgregor——'

But (apart from his own great longing to go back there, 'the strath of his love,' as he called it in one of his own songs, and dear to him for many things) two happenings moved him at last.

First there came word from Donald Macalister of Dalibrog, and that meant much, for Dalibrog was his foster-brother. That is an intimate tender bond; of old, and here and there still, it is a tie closer than blood. 'Fuil gu fichead, comhaltas gu ceud,' as the saying is: 'Blood to the twentieth, fostership to the hundredth degree.'

So that when Donald Macalister wrote affectionately, and addressed him as *comhalta*, Rory's heart melted, and he would have gone to Dalibrog gladly, if only he had not to pass through Strathraonull to get there. 'There are two I want to see, an' badly,' he muttered often: 'my foster-brother and Sheen Macgregor.' Every quarter-day (or as soon after it as he was sober) he had sent Widow Sheen a small packet of tea and tobacco, and the old woman had remembered him gratefully at the New Year, and had sent him a pair of thick hose she had knitted, and a ramshorn mull filled with black snuff that had belonged to her man.

As he could not read or write, and would not own to either lack, he had to wait on opportunity; so that days passed, and Donald Macalister wrote again and urged him by the good bond of *comhaltas* to come to Dalibrog and help make the christening festivities a time for remembrance indeed.

He had received and become acquainted with this second letter, when Peter Macfarlane and Thomas M'Hardy arrived in the carrier's cart at the smithy, and gave Rory one of the proudest moments in his life. For they brought with them a beautiful new set of pipes, with silver flutings, and decked with streamers of M'Alpine tartan, and handed the brave pipes to Rory as a present from the whole of Strathraonull, and as a sign of repentance.

They took back word next day (for that night all three were too overcome with drinking healths, now to Strathraonull, and now to Strathanndra, to stir from the smithy) that Rory M'Alpine was coming to Dalibrog for the christening, and that there was not a man or woman in the Strath but that he would be glad to see again, and that he had not a sour memory left against any one, except for that poor fool of a man, John Macmillan the carpenter (the only man in the Strath who had not subscribed to the new set of pipes), and not that either, seeing the poor home he had with the scolding wife an' a heavy cold in his head three parts o' the year. As for the Reverend Kenneth Maclellan, he had had a call from the Lord, and now preached the Word (at a higher stipend) in the town of Greenock.

II

There never was a finer St. Bride's Eve in the Highlands than that which saw the return of Rory M'Alpine.

He came down by the Pass of the Lochans, at the eastern end of Strathraonull, and long before he was seen the crofters at Creggans could hear the wild pibroch he was playing. A handsome, strapping man he was always; but now he was Piper Rory M'Alpine, and came striding down the pass with his pipes on his left shoulder and skreigh upon skreigh skirling from his chanter and big drone, with the tartan streamers flying in the wind, and himself with a new jacket of braided velveteen with silver buttons and clasps, a new kilt and ~~philabeg~~, new hose of his own clan, with slit and deckled shoes agleam with silver buckles, a great plaid of the finest woven M'Alpine tartan round his big chest and over and away beyond his shoulder, where sat the largest brooch in the Highlands with a yellow cairngorm in it that was like a lump of solid sunlight, and a new cap of the Glengarry men with a sprig of heather held by a silver clasp, which held also two big wing-feathers of the golden eagle.

The whole of Creggans came to the roadside to welcome the glad stranger. He looked at none; but when, still playing his new pibroch, he reached the space in front of the 'Crossways Inn,' he strode backwards and forwards, or stood tapping the ground with his right foot, till the glory and greatness of the man were too overcoming to be borne, and there was a rush of M'Dermids and M'Ians (for every one at Creggans was either a M'Ian or a M'Dermid), and they carried him, just as a running wave sweeps a bit of driftwood, into the laughing gape of the inn.

And what Creggans did, every hamlet along Strathraonull did or tried to do. But as he neared Dálibrog village, Rory became more and more circumspect as to the kindly drink, and so entered the place of his old shame and new triumph with no more in him than what went for comfort. Every man, woman, and child came out to greet him; and what with their laughing glad cries, and shoutings to each other, and the squealing of children and barking of dogs, and the wild ceaseless drone of the pipes and skirling cries that screamed from the chanter, there was noise enough to make the dead in Dalibrog kirkyard wonder if the last trump had sounded, and they not knowing it because of the heavy sleep on them.

It was a triumph indeed, and none ever had a welcome more true. For not only had Rory sent a brave word of thanks for the Strathraonull repentance, and made a beautiful new pibroch (which between Candlemas and Lammas would reach every hamlet in the Highlands from the Mull of Cantyre to the Ord of Sutherland) called 'Strathraonull for Ever!' and had publicly repudiated, too, every curse and ill word he had put on the Strath and the men and women in it; but it was also known that in order to come here in all this glory he had sold the smithy rights to Andrew M'Andrew, the Aberdeen man who had been spying for work in Strathanndra, and was now Piper Rory M'Alpine again, and that and no other.

When he spoke at last, it was like a prince, very cordial and kind.

'Well, well, now,' he said, 'for sure I see well I'm

in dear Strathraonull again. Sure I've never ceased to love it, or the folk within it, and where my heart's been my thoughts have been.'

There was a cheer at that, though every man and woman there knew it was a black lie. But perhaps not that either, and only a good friendly lie.

'It's Macalister land indeed,' Rory added laughingly; for as he glanced about him, he saw that two-thirds at least of the company were of Mhic Alastair. 'Sure we might all as well be in the Isles out yonder'—this in allusion to the fact that some generations ago a number of islesmen (Macleans and Macneils with a few Macdonalds and others) had left the Hebrides and settled on the main, and adopted the clan-name of Macalister because of a famous chieftain whom all claimed as their common ancestor, one Alasdair the Red of Storsay; a matter needless to mention here, were it not that in the region spoken of the people still adhere to certain customs that are Hebridean rather than of the mainland, and of the Southern and Catholic isles at that.

Only too gladly William Macalister of the 'Raonull Arms' would have had Rory as his free guest (and this in despite of all painful memory of the shallowness of the piper's purse in comparison with his deep quenchless thirst); but, as was everywhere understood, he had, of course, to go on to Dalibrog House. But he drank abundant goodwill first.

Dalibrog himself was not an expansive man, but with Rory his *coàlt* he was more cordial than with any other, and had as much affection for him and pleasure in his company as he had in that of any living being after himself; and the more so as Rory never asked anything of him, save bed and board, gladly given, and was, moreover, of poor and humble estate as compared with Donald Macalister of Dalibrog.

But neither Dalibrog nor his wife, nor his old half-sister Dionaid (who still had the Island Gaelic, she having come from Barra in her early womanhood), were pleased when they saw that Rory had already been so eager to show Strathraonull that it had his whole-hearted forgiveness, for he carried too obviously the signs of that repentance and his own overwilling meeting of it more than half-way. It was too wild a tune that he played as he came up Dalibrog House avenue, with a broken crowd at his heels, and himself hating so many uncertain trees running at him, and he trying to play at one and the same time 'The Cock of the North' and 'Deil tak' the Hindmost.'

Rory, however, would not hear a word of reproach, and insisted that he had never been so well in his life, save for a bit of a rheum he had got as he came down the cold pass of the Lochans; and that it would go soon, and quicker too for the help of some good warm broth and a mouthful of something with it (Glenlivet for choice), for he had not touched bite or sup since a slop of porridge and milk at daybreak.

'Well, as ye've enough breath for that lie, I suppose you'll have to reach the end your ain gate,' said Dalibrog drily, and speaking the Lowland tongue to show his displeasure.

However, Rory recovered for a time, and by three of the clock was in a deep sleep in the loft beyond the kitchen, where Dionaid Macalister had given him all he wanted and more. The christening was over and the minister gone before he came out of that sleep, to the thankful content of all concerned.

Meanwhile the St. Bride preparations were carried swiftly on.

The young women of the neighbourhood had already made a fine image of a woman out of woven corn-sheafs, and had clothed this with the best that could be had; and because of the mildness of the winter they had been able to gather many snowdrops and aconites and early daisies, and even primroses and daffodils, and so made the figure of St. Bride like a delight of spring. With brightly-tinted snail shells, and with polished pebbles, and red bramble leaves and golden bracken fronds which had been carefully preserved from October, and with many little ornaments, 'our Brideag dear' was made fair to see.

As soon as the ceremony was over and the great folk gone with the Laird's carriages, the *banal Bride* (the maiden band of St. Bridget) went in procession from cottage to cottage and from house to house. All were young girls, dressed in white, and with their hair down; and as they carried the figure among them, they sang the song of 'Bride bhoidheach oigh nam mile beus' ('Beautiful young Bridget of a thousand charms'); and because none let St. Bride go without an offering, the figure was soon covered with shells and ribbons and flowers and little fineries of all kinds—and many besides gave presents of cheese and cakes and honey, to be given in turn to the poor of the neighbourhood.

When they came to Dalibrog House, old Dionaid Macalister (who many years before was mainly responsible for the St. Bride celebrations in Strathraonull) put a fine white cairngorm in a silver sheath over the heart of the image of St. Bride, which, she said, was for the 'reul iuil Bride,' the guiding star of St. Bridget—that star over the stable at Bethlehem which led St. Bride to the Virgin Mother and her little new-born Son, and made her known and loved for ever as 'Bride nam brat,' St. Bride of the Mantle, for the good deed she did then.

Having ended at Dalibrog, the *banal Bride* made the circuit of the house, and then went to the new byres that had been made ready for the feast, and in the third installed Bridget, 'Bride bhoidheach oigh,' and near the great window where she could be seen of all. Then having barred the doors, they awaited the coming of the other young men and women from the Strath. They came in twos and threes and larger groups; but because most were Protestants, and not of the old faith, and inlanders too, there were songs unsung and prayers unprayed that should have been sung and prayed; nor did more than a few of the young men make obeisance before Bride as they should have done, she being the friend of Mary and the foster-mother of Christ.

After this there was much eating and drinking, though not so much as there seemed, for each put aside something to the common table that was reserved for what was afterwards to be distributed to the poor.

Then the dancing began, and now Rory M'Alpine was again the foremost figure, for there was none in all the home straths or the countries beyond who had so great a store of reels and strathspeys.

He played with magic and pleasure, and had never looked handsomer, in his new grandeur of clothes, and with his ruddy hair aflame in the torch-light, and his big blue eyes shining with a lifting, shifting fire. But those who knew him best saw that he was strangely subdued for Rory M'Alpine, or at least, that he laughed and shouted (in the rare intervals when he was not playing, and there were two other pipers present to help the Master) more by custom than from the heart.

'What is 't, Rory?' said Dalibrog to him, after a heavy reel wherein he had nearly killed a man by swinging upon and nigh flattening him against the wall.

'Nothing, foster-brother dear; it's just nothing at all. Fling away, Dalibrog; you're doing fine.'

Later old Dionaid took him aside to bid him refresh himself from a brew of rum and lemons she had made, with spice and a flavour of old brandy—

'Barra Punch' she called it—and then asked him if he had any sorrow at the back of his heart.

'Just this,' he said in a whisper, 'that Rory M'Alpine's fëy.'

'Fëy, my lad, an' for why that? For sure, I'm thinking it's fëy with the good drink you have had all day, an' now here am I spoiling ye with more.'

'Hush, woman; I'm not speaking of what comes wi' a drop to the bad. But I had a dream, I had; a powerful strange dream, for sure. I had it a month ago; I had it the night before I left Strathanndra; and I had it this very day of the days, as I lay sleepin' off the kindness I had since I came into Strathraonull.'

'An' what will that dream be, now?'

'Sure, it's a strange dream, Dionaid Macalister. You know the great yellow stone that rises out of the heather on the big moor of Dalmonadh, a mile or more beyond Tom-na-shee?'

'Ay, the Moonrock they call it; it that fell out o' the skies, they say.'

'The Yellow Moonrock. Ay, the Yellow Moonrock; that's its name, for sure. Well, the first time I dreamed of it I saw it standing fair yellow in the moonshine. There was a moorfowl sitting on it, and it flew away. When it flew away I saw it was a ptarmigan, but she was as clean brown as though it were summer and not midwinter, and I thought that strange.'

'How did you know it was a ptarmigan? It might have been a moorhen or a——'

'Hoots, woman, how do I know when it's wet or fine, when it's day or night? Well, as I was saying, I thought it strange; but I hadn't turned over that thought on its back before it was gone like the shadow o' a peewit, and I saw standing before me the beautifullest woman I ever saw in all my life. I've had sweethearts here and sweethearts there, Dionaid-nic-Tormod, and long ago I loved a lass who died, Sìne MacNeil; but not one o' these, no, sweet Sìne herself, was like the woman I saw in my dream, who had more beauty upon her than them altogether, or than all the women in Strathraonull and Strathanndra.'

'Have some more Barra punch, Rory,' said Miss Macalister drily.

'Whist, ye old fule, begging your pardon for that same. She was as white as new milk, an' her eyes were as dark as the two black pools below Annora Linn, an' her hair was as long an' wavy as the shadows o' a willow in the wind; an' she sat an' she sang, an' if I could be remembering that song now it's my fortune I'd be making, an' that quick too.'

'And where was she?'

'Why, on the Moonrock, for sure. An' if I hadn't been a good Christian I'd have bowed down before her, because o'—because—well, because o' that big stare out of her eyes she had, an' the beauty of her, an' all. An' what's more, by the Black Stone of Iona, if I hadn't been a God-fearin' man I'd have run to her, an' put my arms round her, an' kissed the honey lips of her till she cried out, "For the Lord's sake, Rory M'Alpine, leave off!"'

'It's well seen you were only in a dream, Rory M'Alpine.'

At another time Rory would have smiled at that, but now he just stared.

'She said no word,' he added, 'but lifted a bit of hollow wood or thick reed. An' then all at once she whispered, "I'm bonnie St. Bride of the Mantle," an' wi' that she began to play, an' it was the finest, sweet, gentle, little music in the world. But a big fear was on me, an' I just turned an' ran.'

'No man 'll ever call ye a fool again to my face, Rory M'Alpine. I never had the thought you had so much sense.'

'She didna let me run so easy, for a grey bitch went yapping and yowling at my heels; an' just as I tripped an' felt the bad hot breath of the beast at my throat, I woke, an' was wet wi' sweat.'

'An' you've had that dream three times?'

'I've had it three times, and this very day, to the tones be it said. Now, you're a wise woman, Dionaid Macalister, but can you tell me what that dream means?'

'If you're really fëy, I'm thinking I can, Rory M'Alpine.'

'It's a true thing: Himself knows it.'

'And what are you fëy of?'

'I'm fëy with the beauty o' that woman.'

'There's good women wi' the fair looks on them

in plenty, Rory; an' if you prefer them bad, you needna wear out new shoon before you 'll find them.'

'I 'm fëy wi' the beauty o' that woman. I 'm fëy wi' the beauty o' that woman that had the name o' Bride to her.'

Dionaid Macalister looked at him with troubled eyes.

'When she took up the reed, did you see anything that frighted you?'

'Ay. I had a bit fright when I saw a big black adder slip about the moonrock as the ptarmigan flew off; an' I had the other half o' that fright when I thought the woman lifted the adder, but it was only wood or a reed, for amn't I for telling you about the gentle sweet music I heard?'

Old Dionaid hesitated; then, looking about her to see that no one was listening, she spoke in a whisper—

'An' you 've been fëy since that hour because o' the beauty o' that woman?'

'Because o' the sore beauty o' that woman.'

'An' it 's not the drink?'

'No, no, Dionaid Macalister. You women are always for hurting the feelins o' the drink. It is not the innycent drink, I am telling you; for sure, no; no, no, it is not the drink.'

'Then I 'll tell you what it means, Rory M'Alpine. It wasn't Holy St. Bride——'

'I know that, ye old——, I mean, Miss Macalister.'

'It was the face of the *Bhean-Nimhir* you saw, the

face of *Nighean-Imhir*, an' this is St. Bride's Night, an' it is on this night of the nights she can be seen, an' beware o' that seeing, Rory M'Alpine.'

'The *Bean-Nimhir*, the *Nighean-Imhir* . . . the Serpent Woman, the Daughter of Ivor——' muttered Rory; 'where now have I heard tell o' the Daughter of Ivor?' Then he remembered an old tale of the isles, and his heart sank, because the tale was of a woman of the underworld who could suck the soul out of a man through his lips, and send it to slavery among the people of ill-will, whom there is no call to speak of by name; and if she had any spite, or any hidden wish that is not for our knowing, she could put the littleness of a fly's bite on the hollow of his throat, and take his life out of his body, and nip it and sting it till it was no longer a life, and till that went away on the wind that she chased with screams and laughter.

'Some say she's the wife of the Amadan-Dhu, the Dark Fool,' murmured Dionaid, crossing herself furtively, for even at Dalibrog it was all Protestantry now.

But Rory was not listening. He sat intent, for he heard music—a strange music.

Dionaid shook him by the shoulder.

'Wake up, Rory, man; you'll be having sleep on you in another minute.'

Just then a loud calling for the piper was heard, and Rory went back to the dancers. Soon his pipes were heard, and the reels swung to that good glad music, and his face lighted up as he strode to and fro, or stopped and tap-tapped away with his right foot, while drone and chanter all but burst with the throng of sound in them.

But suddenly he began to play a reel that nigh maddened him, and his own face was wrought so that Dalibrog came up and signed to stop, and then asked him what in the name o' Black Donald he was playing.

Rory laughed foolishly.

'Oh, for sure, it's just a new reel o' my own. I call it "The Reel of Ivor's Daughter." An' a good reel it is too, although it's Rory M'Alpine says it.'

'Who is she, an' what Ivor will you be speaking of?'

'Oh, ask the Amadan-Dhu; it's he will be knowing that. No, no, now, I will not be naming it that name; sure, I will call it instead the Serpent-Reel.'

'Come, now, Rory, you've played enough, an' if your wrist's not tired wi' the chanter, sure, it must be wi' lifting the drink to your lips. An' it's time, too, these lads an' lasses were off.'

'No, no, they're waiting to bring in the greying of the day—St. Bride's Day. They'll be singing the hymn for that greying, "Bride bhoidheach muime Chriosda."'

'Not they, if Dalibrog has a say in it! Come, now, have a drink with me, your own foster-brother, an' then lie down an' sleep it off, an' God's good blessing be on you.'

Whether it was Dalibrog's urgency, or the thought of the good drink he would have, and he with a terrible thirst on him after that lung-bursting reel of his, Rory went quietly away with the host, and was on a mattress on the floor of a big empty room, and snoring hard, long before the other pipers had ceased piping, or the last dancers flung their panting breaths against the frosty night.

III

An hour after midnight Rory woke with a start. He had 'a spate of a headache on,' he muttered, as he half rose and struck a match against the floor. When he saw that he was still in his brave gear, and had lain down 'just as he was,' and also remembered all that had happened and the place he was in, he wondered what had waked him.

Now that he thought of it, he had heard music: yes, for sure, music—for all that it was so late, and after every one had gone home. What was it? It was not any song of his own, nor any air he had. He must have dreamed that it came across great lonely moors, and had a laugh and a sudden cry in it.

He was cold. The window was open. That was a stupid, careless thing of Donald Macalister to do, and he sober, as he always was, though he could drink deep; on a night of frost like this Death could slip in on the back of a shadow and get his whisper in your ear before you could rise for the stranger.

He stumbled to his feet and closed the window. Then he lay down again, and was nearly asleep, and was confused between an old prayer that rose in his mind like a sunken spar above a wave; and whether to take Widow Sheen a packet of great thick Sabbath peppermints, or a good heavy twist of tobacco; and a strange delightsome memory of Dionaid Macalister's brew of rum and lemons with a touch of old brandy in it; when again he heard that little, wailing, fantastic air, and sat up with the sweat on his brow.

The sweat was not there only because of the little thin music he heard, and it the same, too, as he had heard before; but because the window was wide open again, though the room was so heavy with silence that the pulse of his heart made a noise like a jumping rat.

Rory sat, as still as though he were dead, staring at the window. He could not make out whether the music was faint because it was so far away, or because it was played feebly, like a child's playing, just under the sill.

He was a big, strong man, but he leaned and wavered like the flame of a guttering candle in that slow journey of his from the mattress to the window. He could hear the playing now quite well. It was like the beautiful sweet song of 'Bride bhoidheach muime Chriosda,' but with the holy peace out of it, and with a little, evil, hidden laugh flapping like a wing against the blessed name of Christ's foster-mother. But when it sounded under the window, it suddenly was far; and when it was far, the last circling peewit-lilt would be at his ear like a skiffing bat.

BY THE YELLOW MOONROCK

When he looked out, and felt the cold night lie on his skin, he could not see because he saw too well. He saw the shores of the sky filled with dancing lights, and the great lighthouse of the moon sending a foam-white stream across the delicate hazes of frost which were too thin to be seen, and only took the sharp edges off the stars, or sometimes splintered them into sudden dazzle. He was like a man in a sailless, rudderless boat, looking at the skies because he lay face upward and dared not stoop and look into the dark slipping water alongside.

He saw, too, the horn-like curve of Tom-na-shee black against the blueness, and the inky line of Dalmonadh Moor beyond the plumy mass of Dalibrog woods, and the near meadows where a leveret jumped squealing, and then the bare garden with ragged gooseberry-bushes like scraggy, ~~forlorn~~ hunched sheep, and at last the white gravel-walk bordered with the withered roots of pinks and southernwood.

Then he looked from all these great things and these little things to the ground beneath the window. There was nothing there. There was no sound. Not even far away could he hear any faint devilish music. At least——

Rory shut the window, and went back to his mattress and lay down.

'By the sun an' wind,' he exclaimed, 'a man gets fear on him nowadays, like a cold in the head when a thaw comes.'

Then he lay and whistled a blithe catch. For

sure, he thought, he would rise at dawn and drown that thirst of his in whatever came first to hand.

Suddenly he stopped whistling, and on the uplift of a lilting turn. In a moment the room was full of old silence again.

Rory turned his head slowly. The window was wide open.

A sob died in his throat. He put his hands to his dry mouth; the back of it was wet with the sweat on his face.

White and shaking, he rose and walked steadily to the window. He looked out and down: there was no one, nothing.

He pulled the ragged cane chair to the sill, and sat there, silent and hopeless.

Soon big tears fell one by one, slowly, down his face. He understood now. His heart filled with sad, bitter grief, and brimmed over, and that was why the tears fell.

It was his hour that had come and opened the window.

He was cold, and as faint with hunger and heavy with thirst as though he had not put a glass to his lips or a bit to his mouth for days instead of for hours; but for all that, he did not feel ill, and he wondered and wondered why he was to die so soon, and he so well-made and handsome, and unmarried too, and now with girls as eager to have him as trouts for a may fly.

And after a time Rory began to dream of that great beauty that had troubled his dreams; and while he thought of it, and the beautiful sweet wonder of the woman who had it, she whom he had seen sitting in the moonshine on the yellow rock, he heard again the laughing, crying, fall and lilt of that near and far song. But now it troubled him no more.

He stooped, and swung himself out of the window, and at the noise of his feet on the gravel a dog barked. He saw a white hound running swiftly across the pasture beyond him. It was gone in a moment, so swiftly did it run. He heard a second bark, and knew that it came from the old deerhound in the kennel. He wondered where that white hound he had seen came from, and where it was going, and it silent and white and swift as a moonbeam, with head low and in full sleuth.

He put his hand on the sill, and climbed into the room again; lifted the pipes which he or Donald Macalister had thrown down beside the mattress; and again, but stealthily, slipped out of the window.

Rory walked to the deerhound and spoke to it. The dog whimpered, but barked no more. When the piper walked on, and had gone about a score yards, the old hound threw back his head and gave howl upon howl, long and mournful. The cry went from stead to stead; miles and miles away the farm-dogs answered.

Perhaps it was to drown their noise that Rory began to finger his pipes, and at last let a long drone go out like a great humming cockchafer on the blue frosty stillness of the night. The crofters at Moor

Edge heard his pibroch, as he walked swiftly along the road that leads to Dalmonadh Moor. Some thought it was uncanny; some that one of the pipers had lost his way, or made an early start; one or two wondered if Rory M'Alpine were already on the move, like a hare that could not be long in one form.

The last house was the gamekeeper's, at Dalmonadh Toll, as it was still called. Duncan Grant related next day that he was wakened by the skreigh of the pipes, and knew them for Rory M'Alpine's by the noble masterly fashion in which drone and chanter gave out their music, and also because that music was the strong, wild, fearsome reel that Rory had played last in the byres, that which he had called 'The Reel of the Daughter of Ivor.'

'At that,' he added, each time he told the tale, 'I rose and opened the window, and called to M'Alpine. "Rory," I cried, "is that you?"

'"Ay," he said, stopping short, an' giving the pipes a lilt. "Ay, it's me an' no other, Duncan Grant."

'"I thought ye would be sleeping sound at Dalibrog?"

'But Rory made no answer to that, and walked on. I called to him in the English: "Dinna go out on the moor, Rory! Come in, man, an' have a sup o' hot porridge an' a mouthful with them." But he never turned his head; an' as it was cold an' dark, I said to myself that doited fools must gang their ain gate, an' so turned an' went to my bed again, though I hadn't a wink so long as I could hear Rory playing.'

But Duncan Grant was not the last man who heard 'The Reel of the Daughter of Ivor.'

A mile or more across Dalmonadh Moor the heather-set road forks. One way is the cart-way to Balnaree; the other is the drover's way to Tom-na-shee and the hill countries beyond. It is up this, a mile from the fork, that the Yellow Moonrock rises like a great fang out of purple lips. Some say it is of granite, and some marble, and that it is an old cromlech of the forgotten days; others that it is an unknown substance, a meteoric stone believed to have fallen from the moon.

Not near the Moonrock itself, but five score yards or more away, and perhaps more ancient still, there is a group of three lesser fang-shaped boulders of trap, one with illegible runic writing or signs. These are familiar to some as the Stannin' Stanes; to others, who have the Gaelic, as the Stone Men, or simply as the Stones, or the Stones of Dalmonadh. None knows anything certain of this ancient cromlech, though it is held by scholars to be of Pictish times.

Here a man known as Peter Lamont, though commonly as Peter the Tinker, an idle, homeless vagrant, had taken shelter from the hill-wind which had blown earlier in the night, and had heaped a bed of dry bracken. He was asleep when he heard the wail and hum of the pipes.

He sat up in the shadow of one of the Stones. By the stars he saw that it was still the black of the night, and that dawn would not be astir for three hours or more. Who could be playing the pipes in that lonely place at that hour?

The man was superstitious, and his fears were heightened by his ignorance of what the unseen piper played (and Peter the Tinker prided himself on his knowledge of pipe music) and by the strangeness of it. He remembered, too, where he was. There was not one in a hundred who would lie by night among the Stannin' Stanes, and he had himself been driven to it only by heavy weariness and fear of death from the unsheltered cold. But not even that would have made him lie near the Moonrock. He shivered as memories of wild stories rose ghastly one after the other.

The music came nearer. The tinker crawled forward, and hid behind the Stone next the path, and cautiously, under a tuft of bracken, stared in the direction whence the sound came.

He saw a tall man striding along in full Highland gear, with his face death-white in the moonshine, and his eyes glazed like those of a leistered salmon. It was not till the piper was close that Lamont recognised him as Rory M'Alpine.

He would have spoken—and gladly, in that lonely place, to say nothing of the curiosity that was on him—had it not been for those glazed eyes and that set, death-white face. The man was fëy. He could see that. It was all he could do not to leap away like a rabbit.

Rory M'Alpine passed him, and played till he was close on the Moonrock. Then he stopped, and listened, leaning forward as though straining his eyes to see into the shadow.

He heard nothing, saw nothing, apparently. Slowly he waved a hand across the heather.

Then suddenly the piper began a rapid talking. Peter the Tinker could not hear what he said, perhaps because his own teeth chattered with the fear that was on him. Once or twice Rory stretched his arms, as though he were asking something, as though he were pleading.

Suddenly he took a step or two forward, and in a loud, shrill voice cried—

'By Holy St. Bride, let there be peace between us, white woman!

'I do not fear you, white woman, because I too am of the race of Ivor:

'My father's father was the son of Ivor mhic Alpein, the son of Ivor the Dark, the son of Ivor Honeymouth, the son of Ruaridh, the son of Ruaridh the Red, of the straight unbroken line of Ivor the King:

'I will do you no harm, and you will do me no harm, white woman:

'This is the Day of Bride, the day for the daughter of Ivor. It is Rory M'Alpine who is here, of the race of Ivor. I will do you no harm, and you will do me no harm:

'Sure, now, it was you who sang. It was you who sang. It was you who played. It was you who opened my window:

'It was you who came to me in a dream, daughter

of Ivor. It was you who put your beauty upon me. Sure, it is that beauty that is my death, and I hungering and thirsting for it.'

Having cried thus, Rory stood, listening, like a crow on a furrow when it sees the wind coming.

The tinker, trembling, crept a little nearer. There was nothing, no one.

Suddenly Rory began singing in a loud, chanting, monotonous voice—

> 'An diugh La' Bride
> Thig nighean Imhir as a chnoc,
> Cha bhean mise do nighean Imhir,
> 'S cha bhean Imhir dhomh.'

> (To-day the day of Bride,
> The daughter of Ivor shall come from the knoll;
> I will not touch the daughter of Ivor,
> Nor shall the daughter of Ivor touch me.)

Then, bowing low, with fantastic gestures, and with the sweep of his plaid making a shadow like a flying cloud, he sang again—

> 'La' Bride nam brig ban
> Thig an rigen ran a tom
> Cha bhoin mise ris an rigen ran,
> 'S cha bhoin an rigen ran ruim.'

> (On the day of Bride of the fair locks,
> The noble queen will come from the hill;
> I will not molest the noble queen,
> Nor will the noble queen molest me.)

'An' I, too, Nighean Imhir,' he cried in a voice more loud, more shrill, more plaintive yet, 'will be doing now what our own great forebear did, when he made *tabhartas agus tuis* to you, so that neither he nor his seed for ever should die of you; an' I too, Ruaridh MacDhonuill mhic Alpein, will make offering and incense.' And with that Rory stepped back, and lifted the pipes, and flung them at the base of the Yellow Moonrock, where they caught on a jagged spar and burst with a great wailing screech that made the hair rise on the head of Peter the Tinker, where he crouched sick with the white fear.

'That for my *tabhartas*,' Rory cried again, as though he were calling to a multitude; 'an' as I've no *tuis*, an' the only incense I have is the smoke out of my pipe, take the pipe an' the tobacco too, an' it's all the smoke I have or am ever like to have now, an' as good incense too as any other, daughter of Ivor.'

Suddenly Peter Lamont heard a thin, strange, curling, twisting bit of music, so sweet for all its wildness that cold and hunger went below his heart. It grew louder, and he shook with fear. But when he looked at Rory M'Alpine, and saw him springing to and fro in a dreadful reel, and snapping his fingers and flinging his arms up and down like flails, he could stand no more, but with a screech rose and turned across the heather, and fluttered and fell and fell and fluttered like a wounded snipe.

He lay still once, after a bad fall, for his breath was like a thistledown blown this way and that above his head. It was on a heathery knoll, and he could see the Moonrock yellow-white in the moonshine.

The savage lilt of that jigging wild air still rang in his ears, with never a sweetness in it now, though when he listened it grew fair and lightsome, and put a spell of joy and longing in him. But he could see nothing of Rory.

He stumbled to his knees and stared. There was something on the road.

He heard a noise as of men struggling. But all he saw was Rory M'Alpine swaying and swinging, now up and now down; and then at last the piper was on his back in the road and tossing like a man in a fit, and screeching with a dreadful voice, 'Let me go! let me go! Take your lips off my mouth! take your lips off my mouth!'

Then, abruptly, there was no sound, but only a dreadful silence; till he heard a rush of feet, and heard the heather-sprigs break and crack, and something went past him like a flash of light.

With a scream he flung himself down the heather knoll, and ran like a driven hare till he came to the white road beyond the moor; and just as dawn was breaking, he fell in a heap at the byre-edge at Dalmonadh Toll, and there Duncan Grant found him an hour later, white and senseless still.

Neither Duncan Grant nor any one else believed Peter Lamont's tale, but at noon the tinker led a reluctant few to the Yellow Moonrock.

The broken pipes still hung on the jagged spar at the base. Half on the path and half on the heather was the body of Rory M'Alpine. He was all but naked to the waist, and his plaid and jacket were as torn and ragged as Lamont's own, and the bits were scattered far and wide. His lips were blue and swelled. In the hollow of his hairy, twisted throat was a single drop of black blood.

'It's an adder's bite,' said Duncan Grant.

None spoke.

THE HOUSE OF SAND AND FOAM

WHEN Moira Campbell heard that the man whom she loved and had trusted was to marry the Lady Silis Grant, she left the manse, and went to the linn where the mountain torrent and the glen stream meet.

She sat a long time watching two sulphur butterflies dancing in the sunshine over the clumps of yellow iris which grew on the narrow sandy shores of the river just below the linn. Then she watched a dragon-fly flash like a tiny green and purple arrow from pool to pool. She wondered if it was going to be an early and hot August since the rowan-berries were already bronze, and even here and there scarlet.

Then she remembered that Neil Cameron had written that he was to be married soon. Had he not her troth, she his? She could not understand how such a thing could be. Only a few weeks ago she had told him, there, in that very place, that she had that noon been suddenly startled by the first stir of an all but undreamed-of yet half-dreaded life within. It was here, in this very place, that he had first spoken to her of love. There were a few white clouds that day, and a windhover poising above a scurrying partridge brood; and the wind turned ever the whites of the willow-leaves: she remembered these, and all else.

The strangest thing was that she did not greatly care; that she did not feel. Once, long, long ago, years upon years upon years back it seemed to her, she could remember how sweet it was. She could remember, but she could not feel.

What had happened? Was that killed within her which, once killed, could not live again? Was her soul dead? How could so great a thing—or was it so little a thing, a little wind-worn flame—be so soon, so quickly slain?

She was the same, and yet not the same. Her dress was the same as she wore yesterday; the white kerchief . . . no, she had worn a cherry ribbon at her neck yesterday; and the two tea-roses at the hollow of her neck were fresh plucked, and in her breast, under her dress, was Neil's letter.

How clearly and simply men could write! She smiled, and then looked, startled, at the linn. Why did she smile, she wondered: she forgot.

It was easy for men to say this, to say that. What did truth mean? Her father had often said there was but one truth. It was an easy burden, her heart, now that it was broken. She wondered if all women with broken hearts were like that—she simply did not feel.

Once, when the blind life within her moved, she rose, and stared across the hills with fierce steel-blue eyes. What was it; what was all this bitter cruel wrong done to women, to her, by men, by ... by ... Neil?

A ewe wandered by. A white fluffy lambkin bustled up with a whinnying bleat and tugged at the ready udder.

'Poor little thing!' Moira muttered, then wondered why she thought so, or cared.

She was tired. She did not want to think. Did Neil remember *all* when he wrote?

Soon she was asleep. It was noon when she woke, because of the confused angry hum of a wild-bee tangled in her long sun-brown hair, which had become loosened. She fastened the warm tresses, and flushed at she knew not what. There were too many eyes everywhere. Her breasts felt strained, and hurt her; the roses had too heavy an odour. She rose and looked at the linn. Why was it that circling water made her drowsy? She stared about her, and again a deep flush waved into her pale face. There were too many eyes everywhere: little daisy-eyes, and behind the green fronds of the bracken, and in every little dancing leaf on ash and birch.

When they found her, in the afternoon, on the white sandy reaches tufted with yellow iris, she had been bruised by the brown surging tumult of the linn. In the afternoon shine the foam-bells in her hair, where she lay half in half out the stream, were filled with lovely rainbow-gleams, azure and opal and sudden gold, with little wild-rose flames, breaths of a moment.

LOST

I HAD heard of Mànus Macleod before I met him, a year or more ago, in the South Isles. He had a tragic history. The younger *fiùran* of the younger branch of a noble family, he was born and bred in poverty. At twenty he was studying for the priesthood; nearly two years later he met Margred Colquhoun; when he was twenty-two he was ordained; in his twenty-third year love carried him away on a strong and bitter tide; the next, he was unfrocked; the next again, Margred was dead, and her child too, and Mànus was a wandering, broken man.

He joined, after some years, wherein he made a living none knows how, a band of gypsies. They were not tinkers, but of the Romany clan, the *Treubh-Siubhail* or Wandering Race. He married a girl of that people, who was drowned while crossing the great ford of Uist; for she fell in the dusk, and was not seen, and the incoming tide took her while a swoon held her life below the heart. It was about this time that he became known as Mànus-am-Bard, Manus the poet, because of his songs, and his **Cruit-Spànteach** or guitar, which had belonged to the girl, and upon which she had taught him to play fantastic savage airs out of the East.

He must have been about forty when he became an outcast from the Romanies. I do not know the reason, but one account seems not improbable: that, in a drunken fit, he had tried to kill and had blinded Gillanders Caird, the brother of the girl whom he had lost.

Thereafter he became an idle and homeless tramp, a suspect even, but sometimes welcome because of his songs and music. A few years later he was known as Father Mànus, head of a dirty wandering tribe of tinkers. He lived in the open, slept in a smoky, ill-smelling tent, had a handsome, evil, dishevelled woman as his mate, and three brown, otter-eyed offspring of his casual love.

It was at this period that a lawyer from Inveraray sought him out, and told him that because of several deaths he had become heir to the Earldom of Hydallan: and asked if he would give up his vagrant life and make ready for the great change of estate which was now before him.

Mànus Macleod took the short, black cutty out of his mouth. 'Come here, Dougal,' he cried to one of his staring boys. The boy had a dead cockerel in his hands, and was plucking it. 'Tell the gentleman, Dougal, where you got that.'

The boy answered sullenly that it was one o' dad's fowls.

'You lie,' said his father; 'speak out, or I'll slit your tongue for you.'

'Well, then, for sure, I lifted it from Farmer Jamieson's henyard; an' by the same token ye ca'ed me to do it.'

Mànus looked at the lawyer.

'Now, ye've seen me, an' you've seen my eldest brat. Go back an' tell my Lord Hydallan what you've seen. If he dies, I'll be Earl of Hydallan, an' that evil-eyed thief there would be Master of Carndhu, an' my heir, if only he wasn't the bastard he is. An' neither now nor then will I change my way of life. Hydallan Chase will make fine camping-ground, an' with its fishings and shootings will give me an' my folk all we need, till I'm tired o' them, when others can have them; I mean others of *our* kind. As for the money . . . well, I will be seeing to that in my own way, Mr. What's-your-name. . . . Finlay, are you for saying? . . . Well, then, good-day to you, Mr. Finlay, an' ye can let me know when my uncle's dead.'

I suppose it was about a year after this that I found one day at a friend's house a little book of poems bearing my own surname, with Mànus before it as that of the author. The imprint showed that the book had been issued by a publisher in Edinburgh some twenty years back. It was the one achievement of Mànus, for whom all his kin had once so high hopes, and much of it seems to have been written when he was at the Scots College in Rome. I copied two of the poems. One was called 'Cantilena Mundi,' the other 'The Star of Beauty.' I quote the one I can remember :—

> It dwells not in the skies,
>   My Star of Beauty!
> 'Twas made of her sighs,
> Her tears and agonies,
> The fire in her eyes,
>   My Star of Beauty!
>
> Lovely and delicate,
>   My Star of Beauty!
> How could she master Fate,
> Although she gave back hate
> Great as my love was great,
>   My Star of Beauty!
>
> I loved, she hated, well,
>   My Star of Beauty!
> Soon, soon the passing bell :
> She rose, and I fell :
> Soft shines in deeps of hell
>   My Star of Beauty!

I recalled this poem when, in Colonsay, I met Mànus Macleod, and remembered his story.

He was old and ragged. He had deserted, or been deserted by, his tinker herd; and wandered now, grey and dishevelled, from hamlet to hamlet, from parish to parish, from isle to isle. It was late October, and a premature cold had set in. The wind had shifted some of the snow on the mountains of Skye and Mull, and some had fallen among the old black ruins on Oronsay and along the Colonsay dunes of sand and salt bent. Mànus was in the inn kitchen, staring into the fire, and singing an old Gaelic song below his breath.

When my name was spoken, he looked up quickly.

An instinct made me say this—

'I can give you song for song, Mànus mac Tormod.'

'How do you know that my father's name was Norman?' he asked in English.

'How do I know that as Tormod mhic Leoid's son, son of Tormod of Arrasay, you are heir to his brother Hydallan?'

Mànus frowned. Then he leaned over the fire, warming his thin, gaunt hands. I could see the flame-flush in them.

'What song can you give me for my song—which, for sure, is not mine at all, at all, but the old sorrowful song by Donull MacDonull of Uist, "The Broken Heart"?'

'It is called "The Star of Beauty," I said, and quoted the first verse.

He rose and stooped over the fire. Abruptly he turned, and in swift silence walked from the room. His face was clay-white, and glistened with the streaming wet of tears.

The innkeeper's wife looked after him. 'A bad evil wastrel that,' she said; 'these tinkers are ill folk at the best, and Mànus Macleod is one o' the worst o' them. For sure, now, why should you be speaking to the man at all, at all? A dirty, ignorant man he is, with never a thought to him but his pipe an' drink an' other people's goods.'

The following afternoon I heard that Mànus was

still in the loft, where he had been allowed to rest. He was at death's mouth, I was told.

I went to him. He smiled when he saw me. He seemed years and years younger, and not ill at all but for the leaf of flame on his white face and the wild shine in his great black eyes.

'Give me a wish,' he whispered.

'Peace,' I said.

He looked long at me.

'I have seen the Red Shepherd,' he said.

I knew what he meant, and did not answer.

'And the dark flock of birds,' he added. 'And last night, as I came here out of Oronsay, I saw a white hound running before me till I came here.'

There was silence for a time.

'And I have written this,' he muttered hoarsely. 'It is all I have written in all these years since she died whom I loved. You can put it in the little book you know of, if you have it.' He gave me an old leathern case. In it was a dirty folded sheet. He died that night. By the dancing yellow flame of the peats, while the wind screamed among the rocks, and the sea's gathering voices were more and more lamentable and dreadful, I read what he had given me. But in paraphrasing his simpler and finer Gaelic, I may also alter his title of 'Whisperings (or secret Whisperings) in the Darkness' to 'The Secrets of the Night,' because of the old Gaelic saying, 'The Red Shepherd, the White Hound, and the Dark Flock of Birds: the Three Secrets (or secret terrors) of the Night'—

In the great darkness where the shimmering stars
    Are as the dazzle of the luminous wave
Moveth the shadow of the end of wars :
    But nightly arises, as out of a bloody grave,
The Red Swineherd, he who has no name,
But who is gaunt, terrible, an awful flame
      Fed upon blood and perishing lives and tears;
    His feet are heavy with the bewildering years
Trodden dim bygone ages, and his eyes
Are black and vast and void as midnight skies.

Beware of the White Hound whose baying no man hears,
      Though it is the wind that shakes the unsteady stars :
    It is the Hound seen of men in old forlorn wars :
It is the Hound that hunts the stricken years.
    Pale souls in the ultimate shadows see it gleam
    Like a long lance o' the moon, and as a moon-white
      beam
It comes, and the soul is as blown dust within the wood
Wherein the White Hound moves where timeless shadows
      brood.

Have heed, too, of the flock of birds from twilight places,
    The desolate haunted ways of ancient wars—
Bewildered, terrible, winged, and shadowy faces
    Of homeless souls adrift 'neath drifting stars.
But this thing surely I know, that he, the Red Flame,
    And the White Hound, and the Dark Flock of Birds,
      Appal me no more, who never never again
        Through all the rise and set and set and rise of
        pain
    Shall hear the lips of her whom I loved uttering words,
Or hear my own lips in her shadowy hair naming her
      name.

THE WHITE HERON

It was in summer, when there is no night among these Northern Isles. The slow, hot days waned through a long after-glow of rose and violet; and when the stars came, it was only to reveal purple depths within depths.

Mary Macleod walked, barefoot, through the dewy grass, on the long western slope of Innisròn, looking idly at the phantom flake of the moon as it hung like a blown moth above the ~~vast disclosure of the flower of sunset~~ [lush west]. Below it, beyond her, the ocean. It was pale, opalescent; here shimmering with the hues of the moonbow; here dusked with violet shadow, but, for the most part, pale, opalescent. No wind moved, but a breath arose from the momentary lips of the sea. The cool sigh floated inland, and made a continual faint tremor amid the salt grasses. The skuas and guillemots stirred, and at long intervals screamed.

The girl stopped, staring seaward. The illimitable, pale, unlifted wave; the hinted dusk of the quiet underwaters; the unfathomable violet gulfs overhead;—these silent comrades were not alien to her. Their kin, she was but a moving shadow on an isle; to her, they were the veils of wonder beyond which the soul knows no death, but looks upon the face of Beauty, and upon the eyes of Love, and upon the heart of Peace.

Amid these silent spaces two dark objects caught the girl's gaze. Flying eastward, a solander trailed a dusky wing across the sky. So high its flight that the first glance saw it as though motionless; yet, even while Mary looked, the skyfarer waned suddenly, and that which had been was not. The other object had wings too, but was not a bird. A fishing-smack lay idly becalmed, her red-brown sail now a patch of warm dusk. Mary knew what boat it was—the *Nighean Donn*, out of Fionnaphort in Ithona, the westernmost of the Iarraidh Isles.

There was no one visible on board the *Nighean Donn*, but a boy's voice sang a monotonous Gaelic cadence, indescribably sweet as it came, remote and wild as an air out of a dim forgotten world, across the still waters. Mary Macleod knew the song, a strange *iorram* or boat-song made by Pòl the Freckled, and by him given to his friend Angus Macleod of Ithona. She muttered the words over and over, as the lilt of the boyish voice rose and fell—

> It is not only when the sea is dark and chill and desolate
>   I hear the singing of the queen who lives beneath the ocean :
>   Oft have I heard her chanting voice when noon o'erfloods his golden gate,
>   Or when the moonshine fills the wave with snow-white mazy motion.

And some day will it hap to me, when the black waves are
    leaping,
  Or when within the breathless green I see her shell-strewn
    door,
That singing voice will lure me where my sea-drown'd love
    lies sleeping
  Beneath the slow white hands of her who rules the sunken
    shore.

For in my heart I hear the bells that ring their fatal beauty,
  The wild, remote, uncertain bells that chant their lonely
    sorrow :
The lonely bells of sorrow, the bells of fatal beauty,
  Oft in my heart I hear the bells, who soon shall know no
    morrow.

The slow splashing of oars in the great hollow cavern underneath her feet sent a flush to her face. She knew who was there—that it was the little boat of the *Nighean Donn*, and that Angus Macleod was in it.

She stood among the seeding grasses, intent. The cluster of white moon-daisies that reached to her knees was not more pale than her white face; for a white silence was upon Mary Macleod in her dreaming girlhood, as in her later years.

She shivered once as she listened to Angus's echoing song, while he secured his boat, and began to climb from ledge to ledge. He too had heard the lad Uille Ban singing as he lay upon a coil of rope, while the smack lay idly on the unmoving waters; and hearing, had himself taken up the song—

For in my heart I hear the bells that ring their fatal beauty,
  The wild, remote, uncertain bells that chant their lonely
    sorrow :

*The lonely bells of sorrow, the bells of fatal beauty,
  Oft in my heart I hear the bells, who soon shall know no
   morrow.*

Mary shivered with the vague fear that had come upon her. Had she not dreamed, in the bygone night, that she heard some one in the sea singing that very song—some one with slow, white hands which waved idly above a dead man? A moment ago she had listened to the same song sung by the lad Uille Ban; and now, for the third time, she heard Angus idly chanting it as he rose invisibly from ledge to ledge of the great cavern below. Three idle songs; yet she remembered that death was but the broken refrain of an idle song.

When Angus leaped on to the slope and came towards her, she felt her pulse quicken. Tall and fair, he looked fairer and taller than she had ever seen him. The light that was still in the west lingered in his hair, which, yellow as it was, now glistened as with the sheen of bronze. He had left his cap in the boat; and as he crossed swiftly towards her, she realised anew that he deserved the Gaelic name given him by Pòl the poet—Angus the yellow-haired son of Youth. They had never spoken of their love, and now both realised in a flash that no words were needed. At midsummer noon no one says the sun shines.

Angus came forward with outreaching hands. 'Dear, dear love!' he whispered. 'Mhairi mo rùn, muirnean, mochree!'

She put her hands in his; she put her lips to his;

she put her head to his breast, and listened, all her life throbbing in response to the leaping pulse of the heart that loved her.

'Dear, dear love!' he whispered again.

'Angus!' she murmured.

They said no more, but moved slowly onward, hand in hand.

The night had their secret. For sure, it was in the low sighing of the deep when the tide put its whispering lips against the sleeping sea; it was in the spellbound silences of the isle; it was in the phantasmal light of the stars—the stars of dream, in a sky of dream, in a world of dream. When, an hour —or was it an eternity, or a minute?—later, they turned, she to her home near the clachan of Innisròn, he to his boat, a light air had come up on the forehead of the tide. The sail of the *Nighean Donn* flapped, a dusky wing in the darkness. The penetrating smell of sea-mist was in the air.

Mary had only one regret as she turned her face inland, when once the invisibly gathering mist hid from her even the blurred semblance of the smack— that she had not asked Angus to sing no more that song of Pòl the Freckled, which vaguely she feared, and even hated. She had stood listening to the splashing of the oars, and, later, to the voices of Angus and Uille Ban; and now, coming faintly and to her weirdly through the gloom, she heard her lover's voice chanting the words again. What made him sing that song, in that hour, on this day of all days?

For in my heart I hear the bells that ring their fatal beauty,
  The wild, remote, uncertain bells that chant their lonely
    sorrow:
The lonely bells of sorrow, the bells of fatal beauty,
  Oft in my heart I hear the bells, who soon shall know no
    morrow.

But long before she was back at the peat-fire again she forgot that sad, haunting cadence, and remembered only his words—the dear words of him whom she loved, as he came towards her, across the dewy grass, with outstretched hands—

'Dear, dear love!—mhairi mo rùn, muirnean, mochree!'

She saw them in the leaping shadows in the little room; in the red glow that flickered along the fringes of the peats; in the darkness which, like a sea, drowned the lonely croft. She heard them in the bubble of the meal, as slowly with wooden spurtle she stirred the porridge; she heard them in the rising wind that had come in with the tide; she heard them in the long resurge and multitudinous shingly inrush as the hands of the Atlantic tore at the beaches of Innisròn.

After the smooring of the peats, and when the two old people, the father of her father and his white-haired wife, were asleep, she sat for a long time in the warm darkness. From a cranny in the peat ash a smouldering flame looked out comfortingly. In the girl's heart a great peace was come as well as a great joy. She had dwelled so long with silence that she knew its eloquent secrets;

and it was sweet to sit there in the dusk, and listen, and commune with silence, and dream.

Above the long, deliberate rush of the tidal waters round the piled beaches she could hear a dull, rhythmic beat. It was the screw of some great steamer, churning its way through the darkness; a stranger, surely, for she knew the times and seasons of every vessel that came near these lonely isles. Sometimes it happened that the Uist or Tiree steamers passed that way; doubtless it was the Tiree boat, or possibly the big steamer that once or twice in the summer fared northward to far-off St. Kilda.

She must have slept, and the sound have passed into her ears as an echo into a shell; for when, with a start, she arose, she still heard the thud-thud of the screw, although the boat had long since passed away.

It was the cry of a sea-bird which had startled her. Once—twice—the scream had whirled about the house. Mary listened, intent. Once more it came, and at the same moment she saw a drift of white press up against the window.

She sprang to her feet, startled.

'It is the cry of a heron,' she muttered, with dry lips; 'but who has heard tell of a white heron?—and the bird there is white as a snow-wreath.'

Some uncontrollable impulse made her hesitate. She moved to go to the window, to see if the bird were wounded, but she could not. Sobbing with inexplicable fear, she turned and fled, and a moment later was in her own little room. There all her fear passed. Yet she could not sleep for long. If only she could get the sound of that beating screw out of her ears, she thought. But she could not, neither waking nor sleeping; nor the following day; nor any day thereafter; and when she died, doubtless she heard the thud-thud of a screw as it churned the dark waters in a night of shrouding mist.

For on the morrow she learned that the *Nighean Donn* had been run down in the mist, a mile south of Ithona, by an unknown steamer. The great vessel came out of the darkness, unheeding; unheeding she passed into the darkness again. Perhaps the officer in command thought that his vessel had run into some floating wreckage; for there was no cry heard, and no lights had been seen. Later, only one body was found—that of the boy Uille Ban.

When heartbreaking sorrow comes, there is no room for words. Mary Macleod said little; what, indeed, was there to say? The islanders gave what kindly comfort they could. The old minister, when next he came to Innisròn, spoke of the will of God and the Life Eternal.

Mary bowed her head. What had been, was not: could any words, could any solace, better that?

'You are young, Mary,' said Mr. Macdonald, when he had prayed with her. 'God will not leave you desolate.'

She turned upon him her white face, with her great, brooding, dusky eyes:

'Will He give me back Angus?' she said, in her

low, still voice, that had the hush in it of lonely places.

He could not tell her so.

'It was to be,' she said, breaking the long silence that had fallen between them.

'Ay,' the minister answered.

She looked at him, and then took his hand. 'I am thanking you, Mr. Macdonald, for the good words you have put upon my sorrow. But I am not wishing that any more be said to me. I must go now, for I have to see to the milking, an' I hear the poor beasts lowing on the hillside. The old folk too are weary, and I must be getting them their porridge.'

After that no one ever heard Mary Macleod speak of Angus. She was a good lass, all agreed, and made no moan; and there was no croft tidier than Scaur-a-van, and because of her it was; and she made butter better than any on Innisròn; and in the isles there was no cheese like the Scaur-a-van cheese.

Had there been any kith or kin of Angus, she would have made them hers. She took the consumptive mother of Uille Ban from Ithona, and kept her safe-havened at Scaur-a-van, till the woman sat up one night in her bed, and cried in a loud voice that Uille Ban was standing by her side and playing a wild air on the strings of her heart, which he had in his hands, and the strings were breaking, she cried. They broke, and Mary envied her, and the whispering joy she would be having with Uille Ban. But Angus had no near kin. Perhaps, she thought, he would miss her the more where he had gone. He had a friend, whom she had never seen. He was a man of Iona, and was named Eachain MacEachain Maclean. He and Angus had been boys in the same boat, and sailed thrice to Iceland together, and once to Peterhead, that maybe was as far or further, or perhaps upon the coast-lands further east. Mary knew little geography, though she could steer by the stars. To this friend she wrote, through the minister, to say that if ever he was in trouble he was to come to her.

It was on the third night after the sinking of the *Nighean Donn* that Mary walked alone, beyond the shingle beaches, and where the ledges of trap run darkly into deep water. It was a still night and clear. The lambs and ewes were restless in the moonshine; their bleating filled the upper solitudes. A shoal of mackerel made a sputtering splashing sound beyond the skerries outside the haven. The ebb, sucking at the weedy extremes of the ledges, caused a continuous bubbling sound. There was no stir of air, only a breath upon the sea; but, immeasurably remote, frayed clouds, like trailed nets in yellow gulfs of moonlight, shot flame-shaped tongues into the dark, and seemed to lick the stars as these shook in the wind. 'No mist to-night,' Mary muttered; then, startled by her own words, repeated, and again repeated, 'There will be no mist to-night.'

Then she stood as though become stone. Before her, on a solitary rock, a great bird sat. It was a heron. In the moonshine its plumage glistened white as foam of the sea; white as one of her lambs it was.

She had never seen, never heard of, a white heron. There was some old Gaelic song—what was it?—no, she could not remember—something about the souls of the dead. The words would not come.

Slowly she advanced. The heron did not stir. Suddenly she fell upon her knees, and reached out her arms, and her hair fell about her shoulders, and her heart beat against her throat, and the grave gave up its sorrow, and she cried—

'Oh, Angus, Angus, my beloved! Angus, Angus, my dear, dear love!'

She heard nothing, saw nothing, felt nothing, knew nothing, till, numbed and weak, she stirred with a cry, for some creeping thing of the sea had crossed her hand. She rose and stared about her. There was nothing to give her fear. The moon rays danced on a glimmering sea-pasture far out upon the water; their lances and javelins flashed and glinted merrily. A dog barked as she crossed the flag-stones at Scaur-a-van, then suddenly began a strange furtive baying. She called, 'Luath! Luath!'

The dog was silent a moment, then threw its head back and howled, abruptly breaking again into a sustained baying. The echo swept from croft to croft, and wakened every dog upon the isle.

Mary looked back. Slowly circling behind her she saw the white heron. With a cry, she fled into the house.

For three nights thereafter she saw the white heron. On the third she had no fear. She followed the foam-white bird; and when she could not see it, then she followed its wild, plaintive cry. At dawn she was still at Ardfeulan, on the western side of Innisròn; but her arms were round the drowned heart whose pulse she had heard leap so swift in joy, and her lips put a vain warmth against the dear face that was wan as spent foam, and as chill as that.

Three years after that day Mary saw again the white heron. She was alone now, and she was glad, for she thought Angus had come, and she was ready.

Yet neither death nor sorrow happened. Thrice, night after night, she saw the white gleam of nocturnal wings, heard the strange bewildering cry.

It was on the fourth day, when a fierce gale covered the isle with a mist of driving spray. No Innisròn boat was outside the haven; for that, all were glad. But in the late afternoon a cry went from mouth to mouth.

There was a fishing-coble on the skerries! That meant death for all on board, for nothing could be done. The moment came soon. A vast drowning billow leaped forward, and when the cloud of spray had scattered, there was no coble to be seen. Only one man was washed ashore, nigh dead, upon the spar he clung to. His name was Eachain MacEachain, son of a Maclean of Iona.

And that was how Mary Macleod met the friend of Angus, and he a ruined man, and how she put her life to his, and they were made one.

Her man . . . yes, he was her man, to whom she was loyal and true, and whom she loved right well for many years. But she knew, and he too knew well, that she had wedded one man in her heart, and that no other could take his place there, then or for ever. She had one husband only, but it was not he to whom she was wed, but Angus, the son of Alasdair —him whom she loved with the deep love that surpasseth all wisdom of the world that ever was, or is, or shall be.

And Eachain her man lived out his years with her, and was content, though he knew that in her silent heart his wife, who loved him well, had only one lover, one dream, one hope, one passion, one remembrance, one husband.

CHILDREN OF THE DARK STAR[1]

It is God that builds the nest of the blind bird. I know not when or where I heard that said, if ever I heard it, but it has been near me as a breast-feather to a bird's heart since I was a child.

When I ponder it, I say to myself that it is God also who guides sunrise and moonrise into obscure hearts, to build, with those winged spirits of light, a nest for the blind soul.

Often and often I have thought of this saying of late, because of him who was known to me years ago as Alasdair Achanna, and of whom I have written elsewhere as 'The Anointed Man': though now from the Torridons of Ross to the Rhinns of Islay he is known by one name only, 'Alan Dall.'

No one knows the end of those who are born under

---

[1] This story, and the two which follow, 'Alasdair the Proud' and 'The Amadan,' belong to the series of the Achannas of which three have already appeared: 'The Anointed Man' (*The Sin-Eater* and in *Spiritual Tales*) and 'The Dàn-nan-Ròn,' and 'Green Branches' (*The Sin-Eater* and in *Tragic Romances*).

As to my use of the forename 'Gloom' for the chief personage in these Achanna stories, I should explain that the designation is, of course, not a genuine name in English. At the same time, I have actual warrant for its use; for I knew a Uist man, who, in the bitterness of his sorrow, after his wife's death in childbirth, named his son *Mulad* (*i.e.* the Gloom of Sorrow: grief).

the Dark Star. It is said they are born to some strange, and certainly obscure, destiny. Some are fëy from their youth, or a melancholy of madness comes upon them later, so that they go forth from their kind, and wander outcast, haunting most the lonely and desolate regions where the voice of the hill-wind is the sole voice. Some, born to evil, become, in strange ways, ministers of light. Some, born of beauty, are plumed spirits of decay. But of one and all this is sure: that, in the end, none knows the when or how of their going.

Of these Children of the Dark Star my friend Alasdair Achanna, 'Alan Dall,' was one.

'Alan Dall'—blind, as the Gaelic word means: it was difficult for me to believe that darkness could be fallen, without break, upon the eyes of Alasdair Achanna. He had so loved the beauty of the world that he had forfeited all else. Yet, blind wayfarer along the levens of life as he was, I envied him— for, truly, this beautiful soul had entered into the kingdom of dreams.

When accidentally I met him once again, it was with deep surprise on both sides. He thought I had gone to a foreign land, either the English southlands or 'away beyond.' I, for my part, had believed him to be no longer of the living, and had more than once wondered if he had been lured away, as the saying is.

We spoke much of desolate Eilanmore, and wondered if the rains and winds still made the same gloom upon the isle as when we sojourned there.

We spoke of his kinswoman, and my dear friend, Anne Gillespie, she who went away with Manùs MacCodrum, and died so young; and of Manùs himself and his terrible end, when Gloom his brother played death upon him, in the deep sea, where the seals were, and he hearing nothing, nothing in all the world, but the terror and horror of the Dàn-nan-Ròn. And we spoke of Gloom himself, of whom none had heard since the day he fled from the west —not after the death of Manùs, about which few knew, but after the murder of the swimmer in the loch, whom he took to be his own brother Sheumais and the lover of his desire, Katreen Macarthur. I thought—perhaps it was rather I preferred to think —that Gloom was no longer among the evil forces loose in the world; but I heard from Alasdair that he was alive, and would some day come again; for the men who are without compassion, and sin because it is their life, cannot for too long remain from the place where blooms the scarlet flower of their evil-doing.

Since then I have had reason to know how true was Alasdair's spiritual knowledge—though this is not the time for me to relate either what I then heard from 'Alan Dall,' or what terrible and strange revealing of Gloom Achanna there was some three years ago, when his brother, whom he was of old so wont to mock, was no longer among those who dwell visibly on earth.

But naturally that which the more held me in interest was the telling by Alasdair of how he whom

I had thought dead was alive, and known by another name than his own. It is a story I will tell again, that of 'Alan Dall': of how his blindness came to him, and of how he quickened with the vision that is from within, and of divers strange things; but here I speak only of that which brought him to Love and Death and the Gate of Dreams.

For many weeks and months after he left Eilanmore, he told me, he wandered aimlessly abroad among the Western Isles. The melancholy of his youth had become a madness, but this was only the air that blew continually upon the loneliness of his spirit. There was a star upon his forehead, I know, for I have seen it: I saw it long ago when he revealed to me that beauty was a haunting spirit everywhere: when I looked upon him, and knew him as one anointed. In the light of that star he walked ever in a divine surety. It was the star of beauty.

He fared to and fro as one in a dream, a dream behind, a dream his quest, himself a dream. Wherever he went, the light that was his spirit shone for healing, for peace, for troubled joy. He had ever lived so solitary, so few save his own kin and a scattered folk among the inner isles knew him even by sight, that in all the long reach of the Hebrides from the Butt of Lewis to Barra Head he passed as a stranger—a Gael and an islesman, it is true, because of his tongue and accent, but still a stranger. So great was the likeness he bore to one who was known throughout the Hebrides, and in particular to every man and woman in the South Isles, so striking in everything save height was he to the priest, Father Alan M'Ian, known everywhere simply as Father Alan, that he in turn came to be called Alan Mòr.

He was in Benbecula, the isle of a thousand waters, when he met his brother Gloom, and this on the day or the next day but one following the wild end of Manùs MacCodrum. His brother, dark, slim, shadowy-eyed, and furtive as an otter, was moving swiftly through a place of heather-clumps and brown tangled fern. Alasdair was on the ground, and saw him as he came. There was a smile on his face that he knew was evil, for Gloom so smiled when his spirit rose within him.

He stopped abruptly, a brief way off. He had not descried any other, but a yellowhammer had swung sidelong from a spire of furze, uttering a single note. Somewhere, he thought, death was on the trail of life.

There was motionless stillness for a brief while. The yellowhammer hopped to the topmost spray of the bramblebush where he had alit, and his light song flirted through the air.

Then Gloom spoke. He looked sidelong, smiling furtively; yet his eyes had not rested on his brother.

'Well, now, Alasdair, soon there will not be an Achanna on Eilanmore.'

Alasdair—tall, gaunt, with his blue dreaming eyes underneath his grizzled tangled hair—rose, and put out his right hand in greeting; but Gloom looked beyond it. Alasdair broke the silence which ensued.

'So you are here in Benbecula, brother? I, and others too, thought you had gone across the seas when you left Eilanmore.'

'The nest was fouled, I am thinking, brother, or you, and Manùs too, and then I myself, would not be here and be there.'

'Are you come out of the south, or going there?'

'Well, and for why that?'

'I thought you might be having news for me of Manùs. You know that Anne, who was dear to us, is under the grass now?'

'Ay, she is dead. I know that.'

'And Manùs? Is he still at Balnahunnur-samona? Is he the man he was?'

'No, I am not for thinking, brother, that Manùs is the man he was.'

'He will be at the fishing now? I heard that more than a mile o' the sea foamed yesterday off Craiginnish Heads, with the big school of mackerel there was.'

'Ay, he was ever fond o' the sea, Manùs MacCodrum: fëy o' the sea, for the matter o' that, Alasdair Achanna.'

'I am on my way now to see Manùs.'

'I would not be going, brother,' answered Gloom, in a slow, indifferent voice.

'And for why that?'

Gloom advanced idly, and slid to the ground, lying there and looking up into the sky.

'It's a fair, sweet world, Alasdair.'

Alasdair looked at him, but said nothing.

'It's a fair, sweet world. I have heard that saying on your mouth a score of times, and a score upon a score.'

'Well?'

'Well? But is it not a fair, sweet world?'

'Ay, it is fair and sweet.'

'Lie still, brother, and I will tell you about Manùs, who married Anne whom I loved. And I will be beginning, if you please, with the night when she told us that he was to be her man, and when I played on my feadan the air of the Dàn-nan-Ròn. Will you be remembering that?'

'I remember.'

Then, with that, Gloom, always lying idly on his back, and smiling often as he stared into the blue sky, told all that happened to Anne and Manùs, till death came to Anne; and then how Manùs heard the seal-voice that was in his blood calling to him; and how he went to his sea-folk, made mad by the secret fatal song of the feadan, the song that is called the Dàn-nan-Ròn; and how the pools in the rocky skerries out yonder in the sea were red still with the blood that the seals had not lapped, or that the tide had not yet lifted and spilled greying into the grey wave.

There was a silence when he had told that thing. Alasdair did not look at him. Gloom, still lying on his back, stared into the sky, smiling furtively. Alasdair was white as foam at night. At last he spoke.

'The death of Manùs is knocking at your heart, Gloom Achanna.'

'I am not a seal, brother. Ask the seals. They know. He was of their people: not of us.'

'It is a lie. He was a man, as we are. He was our friend, and the husband of Anne. His death is knocking at your heart, Gloom Achanna.'

'Are you for knowing if our brother Sheumais is still on Eilanmore?'

Alasdair looked long at him, anxious, puzzled by the abrupt change.

'And for why should he not still be on Eilanmore?'

'Have you not had hearing of anything about Sheumais—and—and—about Katreena nic Airt——'

'About Katreen, daughter of Art Macarthur, in the Sleat of Skye?'

'Ay—about Sheumais, and Katreen Macarthur?'

'What about them?'

'Nothing. Ah no, for sure, nothing. But did you never hear Sheumais speak of this bonnie Katreen?'

'He has the deep love for her, Gloom; the deep, true love.'

'H'm!'

With that Gloom smiled again, as he stared idly into the sky from where he lay on his back amid the heather and bracken. With a swift, furtive gesture he slipped his feadan from his breast, and put his breath upon it. A cool, high spiral of sound, like delicate blue smoke, ascended.

Then, suddenly, he began to play the Dannhsa-na-Mairbh—the Dance of Death.

Alasdair shivered, but said nothing. He had his eyes on the ground. When the wild, fantastic, terrifying air filled the very spires of the heather with its dark music—its music out of the grave—he looked at his brother.

'Will you be telling me now, Gloom, what is in your heart against Sheumais?'

'Is not Sheumais wishful to be leaving Eilanmore?'

'Like enough. I know nothing of Eilanmore now. It is long since I have seen the white o' the waves in Catacol haven.'

'I am thinking that that air I was playing will help him to be leaving soon, but not to be going where Katreen Macarthur is.'

'And why not?'

'Well, because I am thinking Katreen, the daughter of Art Macarthur, is to have another man to master her than our brother Sheumais. I will tell you his name, Alasdair: it is Gloom Achanna.'

'It is a cruel wrong that is in your mind. You would do to Sheumais what you have done to Manùs, husband of Anne, our friend and kinswoman. There is death in your heart, Gloom: the blue mould is on the corn that is your heart.'

Gloom played softly. It was a little eddy of evil bitter music, swift and biting and poisonous as an adder's tongue.

Alasdair's lips tightened, and a red splash came

into the whiteness of his face, as though a snared bird were bleeding beneath a patch of snow.

'You have no love for the girl. By your own word to me on Eilanmore, you had the hunger on you for Anne Gillespie. Was that just because you saw that she loved Manùs? And is it so now—that you have a hawk's eye for the poor birdeen yonder in the Sleat, and that just because you know, or have heard, that Sheumais loves her, and loves her true, and because she loves him?'

'I have heard no such lie, Alasdair Achanna.'

'Then what is it that you have heard?'

'Oh, the east wind whispers in the grass; an' a bird swims up from the grass an' sings it in the blue fields up yonder; an' then it falls down again in a thin, thin rain; an' a drop trickles into my ear. An' that is how I am knowing what I know, Alasdair Achanna.'

'And Anne—did you love Anne?'

'Anne is dead.'

'It's the herring-love that is yours, Gloom. To-day it is a shadow here: to-morrow it is a shadow yonder. There is no tide for you: there is no haven for the likes o' you.'

'There is one woman I want. It is Katreen Macarthur.'

'If it be a true thing that I have heard, Gloom Achanna, you have brought shame and sorrow to one woman already.'

For the first time Gloom stirred. He shot a swift, glance at Alasdair, and a tremor was in his white, sensitive hands. He looked as a startled fox does, when, intent, its muscles quiver before flight.

'And what will you have heard?' he asked in a low voice.

'That you took away from her home a girl who did not love you, but on whom you put a spell; and that she followed you to her sorrow, and was held by you to her shame; and that she was lost, or drowned herself at last, because of these things.'

'And did you hear who she was?'

'No. The man who told me was Aulay Mac-Aulay, of Carndhu in Sutherland. He said he did not know who she was, but I am thinking he did know, poor man, because his eyes wavered, and he put a fluttering hand to his beard and began to say swift, stammering words about the herrin' that had been seen off the headland that morning.'

Gloom smiled, a faint fugitive smile; then, half turning where he lay, he took a letter from his pocket.

'Ay, for sure, Aulay MacAulay was an old friend of yours; to be sure, yes. I am remembering he used sometimes to come to Eilanmore in his smack. But before I speak again of what you said to me just now, I will read you my letter that I have written to our brother Sheumais; he is not knowing if I am living still, or am dead.'

With that he opened the letter, and, smiling momently at times, he read it in a slow, deliberate voice, and as though it were the letter of another man:—

Well, Sheumais, my brother, it is wondering if I am dead you will be. Maybe ay, and maybe no. But I send you this writing to let you see that I know all you do and think of. So you are going to leave Eilanmore without an Achanna upon it? And you will be going to Sleat in Skye? Well, let me be telling you this thing: Do not go. *I see blood there. And there is this, too: neither you nor any man shall take Katreen away from me.* You *know that; and Ian Macarthur knows it; and Katreen knows it: and that holds whether I am alive or dead. I say to you: Do not go. It will be better for you and for all. Ian Macarthur is away on the north-sea with the whaler-captain who came to us at Eilanmore, and will not be back for three months yet. It will be better for him not to come back. But if he comes back he will have to reckon with the man who says that Katreen Macarthur is his. I would rather not have two men to speak to, and one my brother. It does not matter to you where I am. I want no money just now. But put aside my portion for me. Have it ready for me against the day I call for it. I will not be patient that day: so have it ready for me. In the place that I am, I am content. You will be saying: Why is my brother away in a remote place (I will say this to you: That it is not further north than St. Kilda nor further south than the Mull of Cantyre!), and for what reason? That is between me and silence. But perhaps you think of Anne some-*

times. Do you know that she lies under the green grass? And of Manùs MacCodrum? They say that he swam out into the sea and was drowned; and they whisper of the seal-blood, though the minister is angered with them for that. He calls it a madness. Well, I was there at that madness, and I played to it on my feadan. And now, Sheumais, can you be thinking of what the tune was that I played?

Your brother, who waits his own day,

GLOOM.

Do not be forgetting this thing: I would rather not be playing the Dannhsa-na-Mairbh. *It was an ill hour for Manùs when he heard the Dàn-nan-Ròn; it was the song of his soul, that; and yours is the Dannhsa-na-Mairbh.*

When he had read the last words, Gloom looked at Alasdair. His eyes quailed instinctively at the steadfast gaze of his brother.

'I am thinking,' he said lightly, though uneasily as he himself knew, 'that Sheumais will not now be putting his marriage-thoughts upon Katreen.'

For a minute or more Alasdair was silent. Then he spoke.

'Do you remember, when you were a child, what old Morag said?'

'No.'

'She said that your soul was born black, and that you were no child for all your young years; and that for all your pleasant ways, for all your smooth way and smoother tongue, you would do cruel evil to man and woman as long as you lived. She said you were born under the Dark Star.'

Gloom laughed.

'Ay, and you too, Alasdair. Don't be forgetting that. You too, she saw, were born so. She said we —you and I—that we two were the Children of the Dark Star.'

'But she said no evil of me, Gloom, and you are knowing that well.'

'Well, and what then?'

'Do not send that letter to Sheumais. He has deep love for Katreen. Let the lass be. You do not love her, Gloom. It will be to her sorrow and shame if you seek her. But if you are still for sending it, I will sail to-morrow for Eilanmore. I will tell Sheumais, and I will go with him to the Sleat of Skye. And I will be there to guard the girl Katreen against you, Gloom.'

'No: you will do none of those things. And for why? Because to-morrow you will be hurrying far north to Stornoway. And when you are at Stornoway you may still be Alan Mòr to every one, as you are here, but to one person you will be Alasdair Achanna, and no other, and now and for evermore.'

Alasdair stared, amazed.

'What wild-goose folly is this that you would be setting me on, you whom it is my sorrow to call brother?'

'I have a letter here for you to read. I wrote it many days ago, but it is a good letter now for all that. If I give it to you now, will you pass me the word that you will not read it till I am gone away from here—till you cannot have a sight of me, or of the shadow of my shadow?'

'I promise.'

'Then here it is: an' good day to you, Alasdair Achanna. An' if ever we meet again, you be keeping to your way, as I will keep to my way: and in that doing there shall be no blood between brothers. But if you want to seek me, you will find me across the seas, and mayhap Katreen—ah, well, yes, Katreen or some one else—by my side.'

And with that, and giving no hand, or no glance of the eyes, Gloom rose, and turned upon his heel, and walked slowly but lightly across the tangled bent.

Alasdair watched him till he was a long way off. Gloom never once looked back. When he was gone a hundred yards or more, he put his feadan to his mouth and began to play. Two airs he played, the one ever running into the other: wild, fantastic, and, in Alasdair's ears, horrible to listen to. In the one he heard the moaning of Anne, the screams of Manùs among the seals: in the other, a terror moving stealthily against his brother Sheumais, and against Katreen, and—and—he knew not whom.

When the last faint wild spiral of sound, that seemed to be neither of the Dàn-nan-Ròn nor of the Dannhsa-na-Mairbh, but of the soul of evil that inhabited both,—when this last perishing echo was no more, and only the clean cold hill-wind came down across the moors with a sighing sweetness, Alasdair rose. The letter could wait now, he muttered, till he was before the peats.

When he returned to the place where he was lodging, the crofter's wife put a bowl of porridge and some coarse rye-bread before him.

'And when you've eaten, Alan Mòr,' she said, as she put her plaid over her head and shoulders, and stood in the doorway, 'will you be having the goodness to smoor the peats before you lie down for the sleep that I'm thinking is heavy upon you?'

'Ay, for sure,' Alasdair answered gently. 'But are you not to be here to-night?'

'No. The sister of my man Ranald is down with the fever, and her man away with mine at the fishing, and I am going to be with her this night; but I will be here before you wake for all that. And so good-night again, Alan Mòr.'

'God's blessing, and a quiet night, good woman.'

Then, after he had supped, and dreamed a while as he sat opposite the fire of glowing peats, he opened the letter that Gloom had given him. He read it slowly.

It was some minutes later that he took it up again, from where it had fallen on the red sandstone of the hearth. And now he read it once more, aloud, and in a low, strained voice that had a bitter, frozen grief in it—a frozen grief that knew no thaw in tears, in a single sob.

You will remember well, Alasdair my brother, that you loved Marsail nic Ailpean, who lived in Eilan-

Rona. You will be remembering, too, that when Ailpean MacAilpean said he would never let Marsail put her hand in yours, you went away and said no more. That was because you were a fool, Alasdair my brother. And Marsail—she, too, thought you were a fool. I know you did that doing because you thought it was Marsail's wish: that is, because she did not love you. What had that to do with it? I am asking you, what had that to do with it, if you wanted Marsail? Women are for men, not men for women. And, brother, because you are a poet, let me tell you this, which is old ancient wisdom, and not mine alone, that no woman likely to be loved by a poet can be true to a poet. For women are all at heart cowards, and it takes a finer woman than any you or I have known to love a poet. For that means to take the steep brae instead of the easy lily leven. I am thinking, Alasdair, you will not find easily the woman that in her heart of hearts will leave the lily leven for the steep brae. No, not easily.

Ah yes, for sure, I am hearing you say—women bear pain better, are braver, too, than men. I have heard you say that. I have heard the whistle-fish at the coming of the tide—but a little later the tide came nearer. And are they brave, these women you who are poets speak of, but whom we who are men never meet! I will tell you this little thing, brother: they are always crying for love, but love is the one thing they fear. And in their hearts they hate poets, Alasdair, because poets say, Be true: *but that cannot be, because women can be true to their lovers, but they cannot be true to love—for love wishes sunrise and full noon everywhere, so that there be no lie anywhere, and that is why women fear love.*

And I am thinking of these things, because of Marsail whom you loved, and because of the song you made once about the bravery of woman. I have forgotten the song, but I remember that the last line of that song was 'foam o' the sea.'

And what is all this about? you will be saying when you read this. Well, for that, it is my way. If you want a woman—not that a man like you, all visions and bloodless as a skate, could ever have that want—you would go to her and say so. But my way is to play my feadan at the towers of that woman's pride and self-will, and see them crumbling, crumbling, till I walk in when I will, and play my feadan again, and go laughing out once more, and she with me.

But again you will say, Why all this? Brother, will you be remembering this: That our brother Marcus also loved Marsail. Marcus is under the wave, you will say. Yes, Marcus is under the wave. But I, Gloom Achanna, am not: and I too loved Marsail. Well, when you went away, you wrote a letter to her to say that you would never love any other woman. She did not get that letter. It is under the old black stone with the carvings on it, that is in the brown water of the bog that lies between Eilanmore farmhouse and the Grey Loch. And once, long afterward, you wrote again, and you sent that letter to Marcus, to take to her and to give to her in person. I found it on the day of his death in the pocket of a frieze coat he had worn the day before. I do not know where it is now. The gulls know. Or perhaps the crabs at the bottom of the sea do. You with your writing, brother: I with my feadan.

Well, I went to Eilan-Rona. I played my feadan there, outside the white walls of Marsail nic Ailpean. And when the walls were crumbling I entered, and I said Come, and she came.

No, no, Alasdair my brother, I do not think you would have been happy. She was ever letting tears come in the twilight, and in the darkness of the sleeping hours. I have heard her sob in full noon, brother. She was fair to see, a comely lass; but she never took to a vagrant life. She thought we were going to Coleraine to sail to America. America is a long way —it is a longer way than love for a woman who has too many tears. She said I had put a spell upon her. Tut, tut. I played my feadan to pretty Marsail. No harm in that, for sure, Alasdair aghrày?

For six months or more we wandered here and there. She had no English—so, to quiet her with silence, I went round by the cold bleak burghs and grey stony towns northward and eastward of Inverness, as far and further than Peterhead and Fraserburgh. A cold land, a thin, bloodless folk. I would not be recommending it to you, Alasdair. And yet, for why not? It would be a good place for the 'Anointed Man.' You could be practising there nicely, brother, against cold winds and cold hearths and bitter cold ways.

This is a long, long letter, the longest I have ever written. It has been for pleasure to me to write this letter, though I have written slowly, and now here, and now there. And I must be ending. But I will say this first: That I am weary of Marsail now, and that, too, for weeks past. She will be having a child soon. She is in Stornoway, at the house of Bean Marsanta MacIlleathain ('Widow M'Lean,' as they have it in that half-English place), in the street that runs behind the big street where the Courthouse is. She will be there till her time is over. It is a poor place, ill-smelling too. But she will do well there: Bean Catreena is a good woman, if she is paid for it. And I paid good money, Alasdair. It will do for a time. Not for very long, I am thinking, but till then. Marsail has no longer her fair-to-see way with her. It is a pity that—for Marsail.

And now, brother, will you be remembering your last word to me on Eilanmore? You said, 'You shall yet eat dust, Gloom Achanna, whose way is the way of death.' And will you be remembering what I said? I said, 'Wait, for I may come later than you to that bitter eating.'

And now I am thinking that it is you, and not I, who have eaten dust.—Your brother,

GLOOM.

And so—his dream was over. The vision of a happiness to be, of a possible happiness—and, for long, it had not been with Alasdair a vision of reward to him, but one of a rarer happiness, which considered only the weal of Marsail, and that whether ultimately he or some other won her—this, which was, now was not: this was become as the dew on last year's grass. Not once had he wavered in his dream. By day and by night the wild-rose of his love had given him beauty and fragrance. He had come to hope little: indeed, to believe that Marsail might already happily be wed, and perhaps with a child's little hands against her breast. I am thinking he did not love as most men love.

When the truth flamed into his heart from the burning ashes of Gloom's letter, he sat a while, staring vaguely into the glow of the peats. There had been a bitter foolishness in his making, he muttered to himself: a bitter foolishness. Had he been more as other men and less a dreamer, had he shown less desire of the soul and more desire of the body, then surely Marsail would not have been so hard to win. For she had lingered with him in the valley, if she had not trod the higher slopes: that he remembered with mingled joy and grief. Surely she had loved him. And, of a truth, his wrought imaginings were not rainbow-birds. Their wings had caught the spray of those bitter waters which we call experience, the wisdom of the flesh. Great love claims the eternal stars behind the perishing stars of the beloved's eyes, and would tread 'the vast of dreams' beneath a little human heart. But there are few who love thus. It was not likely that Marsail was of those strong enough to mate with the great love. The many love too well the near securities.

All night long Alasdair sat brooding by the fire. Before dawn, he rose and went to the door. The hollow infinite of the sky was filled with the incense of a myriad smoke of stars. His gaze wandered, till held where Hesperus and the planets called The Hounds leaped, tremulously incessant, for ever welling to the brim, yet never spilling their radiant liquid fires. An appalling stillness prevailed in these depths.

Beyond the heather-slope in the moor he could hear the sea grinding the shingle as the long, slow wave rose and fell. Once, for a few moments, he listened intent: invisibly overhead a tail of wild geese travelled wedgewise towards polar seas, and their forlorn honk slipped bell-like through the darkness, and as from ledge to ledge of silent air.

As though it were the dew of that silence, peace descended upon him. There was, in truth, a love deeper than that of the body. Marsail—ah, poor broken heart, poor wounded life! Was love not great enough to heal that wound; was there not balm to put a whiteness and a quietness over that troubled heart, deep calm and moonrise over drowning waters?

Mayhap she did not love him now, could never love him as he loved her, with the love that is blind to life and deaf to death: well, her he loved. It was enough. Her sorrow and her shame, at least, might be his too. Her will would be his will: and if she were too weary to will, her weariness would be his to guide into a haven of rest: and if she had no thought of rest, no dream of rest, no wish for rest, but only a blind, baffled crying for the love which had brought her to the dust, well, that too he would take as his own, and comfort her with a sweet, impossible dream, and crown her shame with honour, and put his love like cool green grass beneath her feet.

'And she will not lose all,' he said, smiling gently: adding, below his breath, as he turned to make ready for his departure against the dawn, 'because, for sure, it is God that builds the nest of the blind bird.'

ALASDAIR THE PROUD[1]

'THERE were crowns lying there, idle gold in the yellow sand, and no man heeded them. Why should any man heed them? And where the long grass waved, there were women's breasts, so still in the brown silence, that the flittering moths, which shake with the breaths of daisies, motionlessly poised their wings above where so many sighs once were, and where no more was any pulse of joy.'

'And what was the name of the man who led the spears on that day?'

'He had the name that you have—Alasdair; Alasdair the Proud.'

'What was the cause of that red trail and of the battle among the hills?'

Gloom Achanna smiled, that swift, furtive smile which won so many, and in the end men and women cursed.

'It was a dream,' he said slowly.

'A dream?'

'Yes. Her name was Enya—Enya of the Dark Eyes.'

Alasdair M'Ian's grey-blue eyes wandered listlessly from the man who lay beside him in the heather.

[1] The opening sentence is from the tale in the third section, 'Enya of the Dark Eyes.'

Enya of the Dark Eyes! The name was like a moonbeam in his mind.

Gloom Achanna watched him, though he kept his gaze upon the dry, crackled sprays of the heather, and was himself, seemingly, idly adrift in the swimming thought that is as the uncertain wind.

How tall and strong his companion was! he meditated. Had he forgotten, Gloom wondered: had he forgotten that day, years and years ago, when he had thrust him, Gloom Achanna, aside, and had then with laughing scorn lifted him suddenly and thrown him into the Pool of Dermid? That was in Skye, in the Sleat of Skye. It was many years ago. That did not matter, though. There are no years to remembrance; what was, either is or is not.

And now they had met again by the roadside; and if not in Skye, not far from it, for they were now in Tiree, the low surf-girt island that for miles upon miles swims like a green snake between the Southern Minch and the Hebrid seas. It was a chance meeting too, if there is any chance; and after so many years. Gloom Achanna smiled; a sudden swift shadow it was that crossed his face, smooth, comely, pale beneath his sleek, seal-like dark hair. No, it was not chance this, he whispered to himself; no, for sure, it was not chance. When he looked suddenly at Alasdair M'Ian, with furtive, forgetting eyes, he did not smile again, but the dusky pupils expanded and contracted.

And so, his thought ran, Alasdair M'Ian was a

great man in that little world over yonder, the world of the towns and big cities! He had made a name for himself by his books, his poems, and the strange music wherewith he clothed his words, whether in song or story.

H'm; for that, did not he, Gloom, know many a *dàn,* many a wild *òran*; could he not tell many a *sgeul* as fine, or finer? Ay, by the Black Stone of Iona! Why, then, should this Englishman have so much fame? Well, well, if not English, he wrote and spoke and thought in that foreign tongue, and had forgotten the old speech, or had no ease with it, and no doubt was Sasunnach to the core.

But for all his fame, and though he was still young and strong and fair to see, had he forgotten? He, Gloom Achanna, did not ever forget.

Indeed, indeed, there was no chance in that meeting. Why had he, Gloom, gone to Tiree at all? It had been a whim. But now he understood.

And Alasdair M'Ian—Alasdair the Proud? What was *he* there for? There were no idle, silly folk on the long isle of Tiree to listen to English songs. Ah yes, indeed; of course he was there. Where would he be coming to, after these long seven years, but to the place where he had first met and loved Ethlenn Maclaine?

Gloom pondered a while. That was a strange love, that of Alasdair M'Ian, for a woman who was wife to another man, and he loving her, and she him. She had been the flame behind all these poems and stories which had made him so famous. For seven years he had loved her, and Alasdair the Proud was not the man to love a woman for seven years unless it was out of the great love, which is as deep as the sea, and as wild and hopeless as the south wind when she climbs against the stars.

Then all that he knew, all that he had heard of fact and half fact and cloudy rumour, all that he surmised, became in Gloom's mind a clear vision. He understood now, and he remembered. Had he not heard but a brief while ago that Alasdair was fëy with his love-dream? Did he not know that the man had endured so long, and become what he was, because for all these years he had held Ethlenn's love, because he believed that she loved him as he her? Was it not by this that he lived; that he made beauty with cunning, haunting words? Was it not true that for all her marriage with the good, loving, frail son of Maclaine of Inch, she was in body and mind and soul wife to the man whom, too late, she had met, and who in her had found the bitter infinite way?

Yes; now, in a myriad sudden eddies of remembrance and surmise, he knew the poor tired soul, with its great dreams and imperishable desires, of Alasdair the Proud; and like a hawk his spirit hovered over it, uttering fierce cries of a glad and terrible hate. And of one thing he thought with almost an awe of laughing joy—that, even then, he had upon him the letter which, more than a week before, he had idly taken from Uille Beag, the lad who carried the few letters in that remote place. It was, as he knew, having read it, a letter from Ethlenn to Ronald Maclaine, her husband, who was then in Tiree, and she somewhere in the Southlands, in her and his home. He loved much to play the evil, bitter seduction of his music; that strange playing upon his feadan which none heard without disquietude, and mayhap fear and that which is deeper than fear. But he smiled when he thought of that letter; and the unspoken words upon his lips were that he was glad he had now two feadans, though one was only a little sheet of paper.

For two hours they had walked the same road that day, having met by the wayside. Then, having had milk and some oat-bread from a woman who had a little croft, they had rested on the heather, and Gloom Achanna had told old tales, old tales that he knew would fill the mind of Alasdair M'Ian with ancient beauty, and with the beauty that does not perish, for that which was, being perfect, is proudly enduring with other than mortal breath.

In this way he won his companion to forgetfulness.

For a time there had been a dreaming silence. A pyot called loudly; a restless plover wheeled this way and that, crying forlornly. There were no other sounds, save when a wandering air whinnied in the gorse or made a strange, faint whistling among the spires of the heather.

With a stealthy movement, Gloom Achanna drew his feadan from its clasps beneath his coat. He put the flute to his mouth and breathed. It was as though birds were flitting to and fro in the moonshine, and pale moths of sound fluttered above drowning pools.

Alasdair did not hear, or made no sign. After a time he closed his eyes. It was sweet to lie there, in the honey-fragrant heather, in that remote isle, there where he had first seen the woman of his love; healing-sweet to be away from the great city in the south, from the deep weariness of his life there, from the weariness of men with whom he had so little in common. He was so fevered with the bitter vanity of his love that life had come to mean nothing else to him but the passing of coloured or discoloured moments. If only he might find peace; that, for long, he had wanted more than joy, whose eyes were too sorrowful now.

Out of that great love and passion he had woven beautiful things—Beauty. That was his solace; by that, in that, for that, he lived.

But now he was tired. Too great a weariness had come upon his spirit. He heard other voices than those of Ethlenn whom he loved. They whispered to him by day, and were the forlorn echoes of his dreams.

For Beauty: yes, he would live for that; for his dream, and the weaving anew of that loveliness which made his tired mind wonderful and beautiful as an autumnal glen filled with moonshine. He had strength for this, since he knew that Ethlenn loved him, and loved him with too proud and great a love to be untrue to it even in word or deed, and so far the less in thought. By this he lived.

But now he lay upon the heather, tranced, at rest.

He heard the cold, delicate music float idly above the purple bloom around him. Old fonnsheen, enchanted airs: these, later, Gloom Achanna played. He smiled when he saw the frown passing from Alasdair's brows, and the lines in the face grow shadowy, and rest dwell beneath the closed eyes.

Then a single, wavering note wandered fitfully across the heather; another, and another. An old, sorrowful air stole through the hush, till the sadness had a cry in it that was as the crying of a lamentation not to be borne. Alasdair stirred, sighing wearily. Below the lashes of his eyes tears gathered. At that, Gloom smiled once more; but in a moment watched again, furtively, with grave, intent gaze.

The air changed, but subtly, as the lift of the wind from grass to swaying foliage. The frown came back into Alasdair's forehead.

'Achanna,' he said suddenly, raising his head and leaning his chin against his hand, with his elbow deep in the heather; 'that was a bitter, cruel letter you sent to your brother, Alasdair, that is now Alan Dall.'

Gloom ceased playing, and quietly blew the damp out of his feadan. Then he looked at it sidelong, and slowly put it away again.

'Yes?' he said at last.

'A bitter, cruel letter, Gloom Achanna!'

'Perhaps you will be having the goodness, Alasdair mac Alasdair, if it is not a weariness to you, to tell me how you came to know of that letter?'

'Your brother Alasdair left it in the house of the woman in Benbecula, when his heart was broken by it, and he went north to the Lews, to find that poor woman he loved, and whom you ruined. And there the good priest, Father Ian Mackellar, found it, and sent it to me, saying, "Here is a worse thing than any told in any of your stories."'

'Well, and what then, Alasdair, who is called Alasdair the Proud?'

'Why am I called that, Achanna?'

'Why? Oh, for why am I called Gloom of the Feadan? Because it is what people see and hear when they see me and hear me. You are proud because you are big and strong; you are proud because you have the kiss of Diarmid; you are proud because you have won great love; you are proud because you have made men and women listen to your songs and tales; you are proud because you are Alasdair M'Ian; you are proud because you dream you are beyond the crushing Hand; you are proud because you are (and not knowing that) feeble as water, and fitful as wind, and weak as a woman.'

Alasdair frowned. What word he was going to say died unsaid.

'Tell me,' he said at last, quietly, 'what made you write these words in that letter: "Brother, because you are a poet, let me tell you this, which is old, ancient wisdom, and not mine alone, that no woman likely to be loved by a poet can be true to a poet"?'

'Why did I write that, Alasdair MacAlasdair?'

'Yes.'

'If you read the letter, you know why. I said they were cowards, these loving women whom you poets love, for they will give up all save the lies they love, the lies that save them.'

'It is a lie. It means nothing, that evil lie of yours.'

'It means this. They can be true to their lovers, but they cannot be true to love. They love to be loved. They love the love of a poet, for he dreams beauty into them, and they live as other women cannot, for they go clothed in rainbows and moonshine. But . . . what was it that I wrote? They have to choose at last between the steep brae and the easy lily leven; and I am thinking you will not find easily the woman that in her heart of hearts will leave the lily leven for the steep brae. No, not easily.'

'What do *you* know of love, Gloom Achanna—you, of whom the good Father Ian wrote to me as the most evil of all God's creatures?'

Gloom smiled across pale lips, with darkening eyes.

'Did he say that? Sure, it was a hard thing to say. I have done harm to no man that did not harm me; and as to women . . . well, well, for sure, women are women.'

'It was well that you were named Gloom. You put evil everywhere.'

After that there was silence for a time. Once Achanna put his hand to his feadan again, but withdrew it.

'Shall I be telling you now that old tale of Enya of the Dark Eyes?' he said gently at last, and with soft, persuasive eyes.

Alasdair lay back wearily.

'Yes, tell me that tale.'

'Well, as I was saying, there were crowns lying there, idle gold in the yellow sand, and no man heeded them. And where the long grass waved, there were women's breasts, so still in the brown silence, that the flittering moths, which shake with the breaths of daisies, motionlessly poised their wings above where so many sighs once were, and where no more was any pulse of joy . . .' And therewith Gloom Achanna told the tale of Enya of the Dark Eyes, and how Aodh (whom he called Alasdair the Proud) loved her overmuch, and in the end lost both kinghood and manhood because of her wanton love that could be the same to him and to Cathba Fleet-foot. And with these words, smiling furtively, he ended the tale—

'This is the story of Alasdair the Proud, Alasdair the Poet-King, who made deathless beauty out of the beauty and love of Enya of the Dark Eyes, who sang the same song to two men.'

When Gloom had come to that part of his tale where he told of what the captive woman said to the king, Alasdair slowly turned and again fixed his gaze on the man who spoke, leaning the while on his elbow as before, with his chin in his hand.

When Achanna finished, neither said any word for a time. Alasdair looked at the man beside him with intent, unwavering gaze. Gloom's eyes were lidded, and he stared into the grass beneath the heather.

'Why did you tell me that tale, Gloom Achanna?'

'Sure, I thought you loved *sgeulan* of the old, ancient days?'

'Why did you tell me that tale?'

Gloom stirred uneasily. But he did not answer, though he lifted his eyes.

'Why did you call the man who loved Enya, Alasdair? It is not a name of that day. And why do you tell me a tale little altered from one that I have already told with my pen?'

'For sure, I forgot that. And you called the man . . .?'

'I called him Aodh, which was his name. It was Aodh the Proud who loved Enya of the Dark Eyes.'

'Well, well, the end was the same. It was not a good end, that of . . . Aodh the Proud.'

'Why did you tell me that tale?'

Suddenly Achanna rose. He stood, looking down upon Alasdair. 'It is all one,' he said slowly: 'Aodh and Enya, or Alasdair and Ethlenn.'

A deep flush came into Alasdair's face. A splatch stained his forehead.

'Ah,' he muttered hoarsely; 'and will you be telling me, Gloom Achanna, what you have to do with that name that you have spoken?'

'Man, you are but a fool, I am thinking, for all

your wisdom. Here is a letter. Read it. It is from Ethlenn Maclaine.'

' From Ethlenn Maclaine?'

'Ay, for sure. But not to you: no, nor yet to me; but to Ronald Maclaine her man.'

Alasdair rose. He drew proudly back.

' I will not read the letter. The letter is not for me.' Gloom smiled.

'Then I will read it to you, Alasdair M'Ian. It is not a long letter. Oh no; but it is to Ronald Maclaine.'

Alasdair looked at the man. He said a word in Gaelic that brought a swift darkening into Gloom's eyes. Then, slowly, he moved away.

'A fool is bad; a blind fool is worse,' cried Achanna mockingly.

Alasdair stopped and turned.

' I will neither look nor hear,' he said. ' What was not meant for me to see or hear, I will not see or hear.

'Is there madness upon you that you believe in a woman because she asks you to take her pledged word? Do you not know that a pressed woman always falls back upon the man's trusting her absolutely? When she will be knowing that, she can have quiet laughter because of all her shadowy vows and smiling coward lies that are worse than spoken lies. She knows, or thinks she knows, he will be blind and deaf as well as dumb. It is a fine thing that for a proud man, Alasdair M'Ian! It is à fine thing, for sure! And he is a wise man, oh yes, he is a wise man, who will put all his happiness in one scale of the balance, and his trust in another. It is easy for the woman . . . oh yes, for sure. It is what I would do if I were a woman, what you would do. I would say to the man who loved me, as you love Ethlenn Maclaine, "You must show your love by absolute unquestioning trust." That is how women try to put a cloud about a man's mind. That is how a woman loves to play the game of love. Then, having said that, if I were a woman, I would smile; and then I would go to the other man, and I would be the same with him, and kiss him, and be all tender sweetness to him, and say the same things, and trust him to believe all. It is quite easy to say the same things to two men. I have said to you already, Alasdair M'Ian, that a woman like that is not only untrue to the men who love her, but to love. She cannot say in her heart of hearts, "Love is the one thing." She will say it, yes: first to one, then to the other; and perhaps both will believe. And to herself (she will be sorry for herself) she will say, " I love one for this, and the other for that : they do not clash . . ." knowing well, or perhaps persuading herself so, that this is not a subterfuge. It is the subterfuge of a coward, for she dare not live truly ; she must needs be for ever making up to the one what she gives or says to the other. And you . . . you are a poet, they say ; and have the thing that makes you see deeper and further and surer ; and so it must be you, and not Ronald Maclaine, who will be the one of the two to doubt!' Achanna ceased abruptly, and began laughing.

Alasdair stood still, staring fixedly at him.

'I wish to hear no more,' he said at last quietly, though with a strange, thin, shrill voice; 'I wish to hear no more. Will you go now? if not, then I will go.'

'Wait now, wait now, for sure! Sure, I know the letter off by heart. It goes this way, Alasdair mac Alasdair——'

But putting his hands to his ears, Alasdair again turned aside, and made no sound save with his feet as he trod the crackling undertwigs of the heather.

Gloom swiftly followed. Coming upon Alasdair suddenly and unheard, he thrust the letter before his eyes.

Gloom Achanna smiled as he saw the face of Alasdair the Proud flush deeply again, then grow white and hard, and strangely drawn.

As he did not speak, he muttered against his ears: '*And this is the story of Aodh the Proud, who made deathless beauty out of the beauty and love of Enya of the Dark Eyes, who sang the same song to two men.*'

Still silence.

In a whisper he repeated: 'Who . . . sang . . . the same song . . . to . . . two . . . men.'

A change had come over Alasdair. He was quiet, but his fingers restlessly interwined. His face twitched. His eyes were strained.

'That is a lie . . . a forgery . . . that letter!' he exclaimed abruptly, in a hoarse voice. 'She did not write it.'

Achanna unfolded the letter again, and handed it

H

to his companion, who took it, only in the belief that it was Gloom's doing. Alasdair's pulse leaped at the writing he knew so well. He started, and visibly trembled, when he saw and realised the date. The letter fluttered to the ground. When Gloom stooped to pick it up, he noticed that the veins on Alasdair's temples were purple and distended.

From his breast-pocket Alasdair drew another letter. This he unfolded and read. When he had finished, the flush was out of his white face, and was in his brow, where it lay a scarlet splatch.

He was dazed, for sure, Gloom thought, as he watched him closely; then suddenly began to play.

For a time Alasdair frowned. Then two tears rolled down his face. His mouth ceased twitching, and a blank idle look came into the dulled eyes.

Suddenly he began laughing.

Gloom Achanna ceased playing for a moment. He watched the man. Then he smiled, and played again.

He played the Dàn-nan-Ròn, which had sent Manùs MacOdrum to his death among the seals; and the Davsa-na-Mairv, to which Sheumais his brother had listened in a sweat of terror; and now he played the dàn which is known as the Pibroch of the Mad. He walked slowly away, playing lightly as he went. He came to a rising ground, and passed over it, and was seen no more. Alasdair stood, intently listening. His limbs shook. Sweat poured from his face. His eyes were distended. A terror that no man can tell, a horror that is beyond words, was upon him. When he could hear no more, he turned and looked fearfully about him. Suddenly he uttered a hoarse cry. A man stood near him, staring at him curiously. He knew the man. It was himself. He threw up his arms. Then, slowly, he let them fall. It was life or death; he knew that; that he knew. Stumblingly he sank to his knees. He put out wavering hands, wet with falling tears, and cried in a loud, strident voice.

There was no meaning in what he said. But that which was behind what he cried was, '*Lord, deliver me from this evil! Lord, deliver me from this evil!*'

THE AMADAN[1]

I

THE fishermen laughed when they saw 'The Amadan,' the fool, miscalculate his leap and fall from the bow of the smack *Tonn* into the shallows. He splashed clumsily, and stared in fear, now at the laughing men, now at the shore.

Stumbling, he waded through the shallows. A gull wheeled above his head, screaming. He screamed back. The men in the *Tonn* laughed.

The Amadan was tall, and seemed prematurely bent; his hair was of a dusty white, though he had not the look of age, but of a man in the prime of life.

It was not a month since Gloom Achanna had played madness upon him. Now, none of his Southland friends would have recognised Alasdair M'Ian, Alasdair the Proud. His clothes were torn and soiled; his mien was wild and strange; but the change was from within. The spirit of the man had looked into hell. That was why Alasdair the Proud had become 'The Amadan,' the wandering fool.

It was a long way from Tiree to Askaig in the Lews, or the Long Island, as the Hebrideans call it.

[1] Pronounce Ŏmădāĭn.

Alasdair had made Peter Macaulay laugh by saying that he had been sailing, sailing, from Tiree for a hundred years.

When he stood upon the dry sand, he looked at the smack wonderingly. He waved his hand.

'Where . . . where . . . is Tiree?' he cried. The men laughed at the question and at his voice. Suddenly old Ewan MacEwan rose and took his pipe from his mouth.

'That will do now, men, for sure,' he said quietly. 'It is God that did that. We have laughed too much.'

'Oh,' answered Peter Macaulay, abashed, 'he is only an *amadan*. He does not know whether we laugh or why.'

'God knows.'

'Ay, ay, for sure. Well, to be sure, yes, you will be right in what you say, Ewan.'

With that, Macaulay made as though he would call to the man; but the old man, who was skipper, put him aside.

Ewan went to the bow, and slid over by a rope. He stood for a moment in his sea-boots, with the tide-wash reaching to his knees. Then he waded to the shore and went up to the man who was a fool.

'Tell me, poor man, what is your name.'

'Enya.'

'Ay, that is all you will say. But that is not a man's name. It is a woman's name that. Tell me your name, poor man.'

'Enya—Enya of the Dark Eyes.'

'No, no, now, for sure, you said it was Aodh.'

'Yes; Aodh. Aodh the Proud.'

'Ah, for sure, may God give you peace, poor soul! It is a poor pride, I am fearing.'

The man did not answer.

'And have you no thought now of where you will be going?'

'Yes . . . no . . . yes . . . there is a star in the west.'

'Have you any money, poor man? Well, now, see here; here is a little money. It is a shilling and two pennies. It is all I have. But I have my mind, and God is good. Will you be caring, now, to have my pipe, poor man? A good smoke is a peaceful thing: yes, now, here is my pipe. Take it, take it!'

But Alasdair M'Ian only shook his head. He took the money and looked at it. A troubled look came into his face. Suddenly there were tears in his eyes.

'I remember . . . I remember . . .' he began, stammeringly. 'It is an old saying. It is . . . it is God . . . that builds . . . it is God that builds the nest . . . of the blind bird.'

Ewan MacEwan took off his blue bonnet. Then he looked up into the great terrible silence. God heard.

Before he spoke again, a man came over the high green-laced dune which spilt into the machar beyond the shore. He was blind, and was led by a dog.

Ewan gave a sigh of relief. He knew the man.

It was Alan Dall. There would be help now for the Amadan, if help there could be.

He went towards the blind man, who stopped when he heard steps. 'How tall and thin he was!' thought Ewan. His long, fair hair, streaked with grey, hung almost to his shoulders. His pale face was lit by the beauty of his spirit. It shone like a lamp. Blind though he was, there was a strange living light in his blue eyes.

'Who is it?' he asked, in the Gaelic, and in a voice singularly low and sweet.

'Who is it? I was lying asleep in the warm sand when I heard laughter.'

Ewan MacEwan went close to him, and told all he had to tell.

When he was done, Alan Dall spoke.

'Leave the poor man with me, Ewan my friend. I will guide him to a safe place, and mayhap Himself, to whom be praise, will build the nest that he seeks, blind bird that he is.'

And so it was.

It was not till the third day that Alan Dall knew who the Amadan was.

A heavy rain had fallen since morning. Outside the turf bothie where Alan Dall had his brief home, a ceaseless splash made a drowsy peace like the humming of bees. Through it moved in sinuous folds of sound a melancholy sighing; the breathing of the tide wearily lifting and falling among the heavy masses of wrack which clothed the rocks of the inlet above which the bothie stood.

Since he had eaten of the porridge and milk and coarse bread, brought him by the old woman who came every morning to see to his fire and food, Alan Dall had sat before the peats, brooding upon many things, things of the moment, and the deep insatiable desires of the hungry spirit; but most upon the mystery of the man whom he had brought thither. He slept still, the poor Amadan. It was well; he would not arouse him. The sound of the rain had deep rest in it.

The night before, the Amadan, while staring into the red heart of the peats, had suddenly stirred.

'What is it?' Alan had asked gently.

'My name is Alasdair.'

'Alasdair? I too . . . I know well one who is named Alasdair.'

'Is he called Alasdair the Proud?'

'No; he is not called the Proud.'

'You have told me that your name is Alan?'

'Ay. I am called Alan Dall because I am blind.'

'I have seen your face before, or in a dream, Alan Dall.'

'And what will your father's name be, and the name of your father's fathers?'

'I do not know that name, nor the name of my clan.'

Thereupon a long silence had fallen. Thrice Alan

spoke, but the Amadan either did not hear, or would make no answer.

An eddy of wind rose and fell. The harsh screaming cry of a heron rent the silence. Then there was silence again.

The Amadan stirred restlessly.

'Who was that?' he asked in a whisper.

'It was no one, Alasdair my friend.'

Alasdair rose and stealthily went to the door. He lifted the latch and looked out.

The dog followed him, whimpering.

'*Hush-sh, Sùil!*' whispered Alan Dall.

The dog slipped beyond Alasdair. He put back his ears, and howled.

Alan rose and went to the Amadan, and took him by the sleeve, and so led him back to the stool before the glowing peats.

'Who did you think it was?' he asked, when the Amadan was seated again, and no longer trembled.

'Who was it, Alan Dall?'

'It was a heron.'

'They say herons that cry by night are people out of the grave.'

'It may be so. But there is no harm to them that hear if it is not their hour.'

'It was like a man laughing.'

'Who would laugh, here, in this lonely place, and at night; and for why?'

'I know a man who would laugh here, in this lonely place, and at night, and for why too.'

'Who?'

'His name is Gloom.'

Alan Dall started. A quiver passed over his face, and his hand trembled.

'That is a strange name for a man, *Gruaim*. I have heard only of one man who bore that name.'

'There can be only one man. His name is Gloom Achanna.'

'Gruaim Achanna. Yes . . . I know the man.'

He would not tell the Amadan that this man was his brother; or not yet. He too, then, poor fool, had been caught in the mesh of that evil. And now, perhaps, he would be able to see through the mystery which beset this man whom he had taken to guard and to heal.

But Alasdair M'Ian said one saying only, and would speak no more; and that saying was, 'He is not a man; he is a devil.' Soon after this the Amadan suddenly lapsed into a swoon of sleep, even while words were stammering upon his lips.

But now Alan Dall understood better. A deeper pity, too, was in his heart. This poor man, this Amadan, was indeed his comrade, if his cruel sorrow had come to him through Gloom Achanna.

When he rose in the morning at the first sobbing of the rainy wind, and saw how profoundly the Amadan slept, he did not wake him.

Thus it was that throughout that long day Alan Dall sat, pondering and dreaming before the peats, while Alasdair the Proud lay drowned in sleep.

The day darkened early, because of the dense

mists which came out of the sea and floated heavily between the myriad grey reeds of the rain and the fluent green and brown which was the ground.

With the dusk the Amadan stirred. Alan Dall crossed to the inset bed, and stood listening intently.

Alasdair muttered strangely in his sleep; and though he had hitherto, save for a few words, spoken in the English tongue, he now used the Gaelic. The listener caught fragments only . . . *an Athair Uibhreach*, the Haughty Father . . . *Agus thug e aoradh dha*, and worshipped him . . . *Biodh uachdaranachd aca*, let them have dominion.

'Those evil ones that go with Gloom my brother,' he muttered; 'those evil spirits have made their kingdom among his dreams.'

'Who are they who are about you?' he whispered.

The Amadan turned, and his lips moved. But it was as though others spoke through him—

'*Cha 'n ann do Shiol Adhamh sinn,*
Ach tha sinn de mhuinntir an Athar Uaibhrich.'[1]

Alan Dall hesitated. One of the white prayers of Christ was on his lips, but he remembered also the old wisdom of his fathers. So he kneeled, and said a *seun*, that is strong against the bitter malice of demoniac wiles.

Thereafter he put upon him this *eolas* of healing,

---

[1] *We are not of the seed of Adam,*
But we are the offspring of the Haughty Father.

touching the brow and the heart as he said *here* and *here*—

> 'Deep peace I breathe into you,
> O weariness, here:
> O ache, here!
> Deep peace, a soft white dove to you;
> Deep peace, a quiet rain to you;
> Deep peace, an ebbing wave to you!
> Deep peace, red wind of the east from you;
> Deep peace, grey wind of the west to you;
> Deep peace, dark wind of the north from you;
> Deep peace, blue wind of the south to you!
> Deep peace, pure red of the flame to you;
> Deep peace, pure white of the moon to you;
> Deep peace, pure green of the grass to you;
> Deep peace, pure brown of the earth to you;
> Deep peace, pure grey of the dew to you,
> Deep peace, pure blue of the sky to you!
> Deep peace of the running wave to you,
> Deep peace of the flowing air to you,
> Deep peace of the quiet earth to you,
> Deep peace of the sleeping stones to you!
> Deep peace of the Yellow Shepherd to you,
> Deep peace of the Wandering Shepherdess to you,
> Deep peace of the Flock of Stars to you,
> Deep peace from the Son of Peace to you,
> Deep peace from the heart of Mary to you,
> And from Bridget of the Mantle
> Deep peace, deep peace!
> And with the kindness too of the Haughty Father,
> Peace!
> In the name of the Three who are One,
> Peace!
> And by the will of the King of the Elements,
> Peace! Peace!'

Then, for a time he prayed: and, as he prayed, a white and beautiful Image stood beside him, and put soft moonwhite hands upon the brow of the Amadan.

In this wise the beauty of Alan Dall's spirit, that had become a prayer, was created by God into a new immortal spirit.

The Image was as a wavering reed of light, before it stooped and kissed the soul of Alasdair, and was at one with it.

Alasdair opened his eyes. God had healed him.

THE HERDSMAN

I

ON the night when Alan Carmichael with his old servant and friend, Ian M'Ian, arrived in Balnaree ('Baile'-na-Righ'), the little village wherein was all that Borosay had to boast of in the way of civic life, he could not disguise from himself that he was regarded askance.

Rightly or wrongly, he took this to be resentment because of his having wed (alas, he recalled, wed and lost) the daughter of the man who had killed Ailean Carmichael in a duel. So possessed was he by this idea, that he did not remember how little likely the islanders were to know anything of him or his beyond the fact that Ailean MacAlasdair Rhona had died abroad.

The trouble became more than an imaginary one when, on the morrow, he tried to find a boat for the passage to Rona. But for the Frozen Hand, as the triple-peaked hill to the south of Balnaree was called, Rona would have been visible; nor was it, with a fair wind, more than an hour's sail distant.

Nevertheless, he could detect in every one to

whom he spoke a strange reluctance. At last he asked an old man of his own surname why there was so much difficulty.

In the island way, Sheumas Carmichael replied that the people on Elleray, the island adjacent to Rona, were unfriendly.

'But unfriendly at what?'

'Well, at this and at that. But for one thing, they are not having any dealings with the Carmichaels. They are all Macneils there, Macneils of Barra. There is a feud, I am thinking; though I know nothing of it; no, not I.'

'But Sheumas mac Eachainn, you know well yourself that there are almost no Carmichaels to have a feud with! There are you and your brother, and there is your cousin over at Sgòrr-Bhan on the other side of Borosay Who else is there?'

To this the man could say nothing. Distressed, Alan sought Ian and bade him find out what he could. He also was puzzled and uneasy. That some evil was at work could not be doubted, and that it was secret boded ill.

Ian was a stranger in Borosay because of his absence since boyhood; but, after all, Ian mac Iain mhic Dhonuill was to the islanders one of themselves; and though he came there with a man under a shadow (though this phrase was not used in Ian's hearing), that was not his fault.

And when he reminded them that for these many years he had not seen the old woman, his sister Giorsal; and spoke of her, and of their long separation, and of his wish to see her again before he died, there was no more hesitation, but only kindly willingness to help.

Within an hour a boat was ready to take the homefarers to the Isle of Caves, as Rona is sometimes called. Before the hour was gone, they, with the stores of food and other things, were slipping seaward out of Borosay Haven.

The moment the headland was rounded, the heights of Rona came into view. Great gaunt cliffs they are, precipices of black basalt; though on the south side they fall away in grassy declivities which hang a greenness over the wandering wave for ever sobbing round that desolate shore. But it was not till the Sgòrr-Dhu, a conical black rock at the south-east end of the island, was reached, that the stone keep, known as Caisteal-Rhona, came in sight.

It stands at the landward extreme of a rocky ledge, on the margin of a green *àiridh*. Westward is a small dark-blue sea loch, no more than a narrow haven. To the north-west rise precipitous cliffs; northward, above the green pasture and a stretch of heather, is a woodland belt of some three or four hundred pine-trees. It well deserves its poetic name of I-monair, as Aodh the Islander sang of it; for it echoes ceaselessly with wind and wave. If the waves dash against it from the south or east, a loud crying is upon the faces of the rocks; if from the north or north-east, there are unexpected inland silences, but amid the pines a continual voice. It is when the wind blows from the south-west, or the huge

Atlantic billows surge out of the west, that Rona is given over to an indescribable tumult. Through the whole island goes the myriad echo of a continuous booming; and within this a sound as though waters were pouring through vast hidden conduits in the heart of every precipice, every rock, every boulder. This is because of the sea-arcades of which it consists, for from the westward the island has been honeycombed by the waves. No living man has ever traversed all those mysterious, winding sea-galleries. Many have perished in the attempt. In the olden days the Uisteans and Barrovians sought refuge there from the marauding Danes and other pirates out of Lochlin; and in the time when the last Scottish king took shelter in the west, many of his island followers found safety among these perilous arcades.

Some of them reach an immense height. These are filled with a pale green gloom which in fine weather, and at noon or toward sundown, becomes almost radiant. But most have only a dusky green obscurity, and some are at all times dark with a darkness that has seen neither sun nor moon nor star for unknown ages. Sometimes, there, a phosphorescent wave will spill a livid or a cold blue flame, and for a moment a vast gulf of dripping basalt be revealed; but day and night, night and day, from year to year, from age to age, that awful wave-clamant darkness is unbroken.

To the few who know some of the secrets of the passages, it is possible, except when a gale blows from any quarter but the north, to thread these dim arcades in a narrow boat, and so to pass from the Hebrid Seas to the outer Atlantic. But for the unwary there might well be no return; for in that maze of winding galleries and sea-washed, shadowy arcades, confusion is but another name for death. Once bewildered, there is no hope; and the lost adventurer will remain there idly drifting from barren passage to passage, till he perish of hunger and thirst, or, maddened by the strange and appalling gloom and the unbroken silence—for there the muffled voice of the sea is no more than a whisper—leap into the green waters which for ever slide stealthily from ledge to ledge.

Now, as Alan approached his remote home, he thought of these death-haunted corridors, avenues of the grave, as they are called in the 'Cumha Fhir-Mearanach Aonghas mhic Dhonuill'—the Lament of mad Angus Macdonald.

When at last the unwieldy brown coble sailed into the little haven, it was to create unwonted excitement among the few fishermen who put in there frequently for bait. A group of eight or ten was upon the rocky ledge beyond Caisteal-Rhona, among them the elderly woman who was sister to Ian mac Iain.

At Alan's request, Ian went ashore in advance in a small punt. He was to wave his hand if all were well, for Alan could not but feel apprehensive on account of the strange ill-will that had shown itself at Borosay.

It was with relief that he saw the signal when, after Ian had embraced his sister, and shaken hands with all the fishermen, he had explained that the son of Ailean Carmichael was come out of the south, and had come to live a while at Caisteal-Rhona.

All there uncovered and waved their hats. Then a shout of welcome went up, and Alan's heart was glad. But the moment he had set foot on land he saw a startled look come into the eyes of the fishermen—a look that deepened swiftly into one of aversion, almost of fear.

One by one the men moved away, awkward in their embarrassment. Not one came forward with outstretched hand, or said a word of welcome.

At first amazed, then indignant, Ian reproached them. They received his words in ashamed silence. Even when with a bitter tongue he taunted them, they answered nothing.

'Giorsal,' said Ian, turning in despair to his sister, 'is it madness that you have?'

But even she was no longer the same. Her eyes were fixed upon Alan with a look of dread, and indeed of horror. It was unmistakable, and Alan himself was conscious of it, with a strange sinking of the heart. 'Speak, woman!' he demanded. 'What is the meaning of this thing? Why do you and these men look at me askance?'

'God forbid!' answered Giorsal Macdonald with white lips; 'God forbid that we look at the son of Ailean Carmichael askance. But——'

'But what?'

With that the woman put her apron over her head and moved away, muttering strange words.

'Ian, what is this mystery?'

'How am I for knowing, Alan mac Ailean? It is all a darkness to me also. But I will be finding that out soon.'

That, however, was easier for Ian to say than to do. Meanwhile, the brown coble tacked back to Borosay, and the fishermen sailed away to the Barra coasts, and Alan and Ian were left solitary in their wild and remote home.

But in that very solitude Alan found healing. From what Giorsal hinted, he came to believe that the fishermen had experienced one of those strange dream-waves which, in remote isles, occur at times, when whole communities will be wrought by the self-same fantasy. When day by day went past, and no one came near, he at first was puzzled, and even resentful; but this passed, and soon he was glad to be alone. Ian, however, knew that there was another cause for the inexplicable aversion that had been shown. But he was silent, and kept a patient watch for the hour that the future held in its shroud. As for Giorsal, she was dumb; but no more looked at Alan askance.

And so the weeks went. Occasionally a fishing smack came with the provisions, for the weekly despatch of which Alan had arranged at Loch Boisdale, and sometimes the Barra men put in at the haven, though they would never stay long, and always avoided Alan as much as was possible.

In that time Alan and Ian came to know and love

their strangely beautiful island home. Hours and hours at a time they spent exploring the dim, green, winding sea-galleries, till at last they knew the chief arcades thoroughly.

They had even ventured into some of the narrow, snake-like inner passages, but never for long, because of the awe and dread these held, silent estuaries of the grave.

Week after week passed, and to Alan it was as the going of the grey owl's wing, swift and silent.

Then it was that, on a day of the days, he was suddenly stricken with a new and startling dread.

II

In the hour that this terror came upon him Alan was alone upon the high slopes of Rona, where the grass fails and the lichen yellows at close on a thousand feet above the sea.

The day had been cloudless since sunrise. The sea was as the single vast petal of an azure flower, all of one unbroken blue save for the shadows of the scattered isles and the slow-drifting mauve or purple of floating weed. Countless birds congregated from every quarter. Guillemots and puffins, cormorants and northern divers, everywhere darted, swam, or slept upon the listless ocean, whose deep breathing no more than lifted a league-long calm here and there, to lapse breathlike as it rose. Through the not less silent quietudes of air the grey skuas swept with curving flight, and the narrow-winged terns made a constant white shimmer. At remote altitudes the gannet motionlessly drifted. Oceanward the great widths of calm were rent now and again by the shoulders of the porpoises which followed the herring trail, their huge, black, revolving bodies looming large above the silent wave. Not a boat was visible anywhere; not even upon the most distant horizons did a brown sail fleck itself duskily against the skyward wall of steely blue.

In the great stillness which prevailed, the noise of the surf beating around the promontory of Aonaig was audible as a whisper; though even in that windless hour the confused rumour of the sea, moving through the arcades of the island, filled the hollow of the air overhead. Ever since the early morning Alan had moved under a strange gloom. Out of that golden glory of midsummer a breath of joyous life should have reached his heart, but it was not so. For sure, there is sometimes in the quiet beauty of summer an air of menace, a premonition of suspended force—a force antagonistic and terrible. All who have lived in these lonely isles know the peculiar intensity of this summer melancholy. No noise of wind, no prolonged season of untimely rains, no long baffling of mists in all the drear inclemencies of that remote region, can produce the same ominous and even paralysing gloom sometimes born of ineffable peace and beauty. Is it that in the human soul there is mysterious kinship with the outer soul which we call Nature; and that in these few supreme hours which come at the full of the year, we are, sometimes, suddenly aware of the tremendous forces beneath and behind us, momently quiescent?

Determined to shake off this dejection, Alan wandered high among the upland solitudes. There a cool air moved always, even in the noons of August; and there, indeed, often had come upon him a deep peace. But whatsoever the reason, only a deeper despondency possessed him. An incident, significant in that mood, at that time, happened then. A few hundred yards away from where he stood, half hidden in a little glen where a fall of water tossed its spray among the shadows of rowan and birch, was the bothie of a woman, the wife of Neil MacNeill, a fisherman of Aonaig. She was there, he knew, for the summer pasturing; and even as he recollected this, he heard the sound of her voice as she sang somewhere by the burnside. Moving slowly toward the corrie, he stopped at a mountain ash which overhung a pool. Looking down, he saw the woman, Morag MacNeill, washing and peeling potatoes in the clear brown water. And as she washed and peeled, she sang an old-time shealing hymn of the Virgin-Shepherdess, of Michael the White, and of Columan the Dove. It was a song that, years ago, far away in Brittany, he had heard from his mother's lips. He listened now to every word of the doubly familiar Gaelic; and when Morag ended, the tears were in his eyes, and he stood for a while as one under a spell[1]—

> 'A Mhicheil mhin ! nan steud geala,
> A choisin cios air Dragon fala,
> Air ghaol Dia 'us Mhic Muire,
> Sgaoil do sgiath oirnn dian sinn uile,
> Sgaoil do sgiath oirnn dian sinn uile.
>
> A Mhoire ghradhach ! Mathair Uain-ghil,
> Cobhair oirnne, Oigh na h-uaisle ;
> A rioghainn uai'reach ! a bhuachaille nan treud !
> Cum ar cuallach cuartaich sinn le cheil,
> Cum ar cuallach cuartaich sinn le cheil.
>
> A Chalum-Chille ! chairdeil, chaoimh,
> An ainm Athar, Mic, 'us Spioraid Naoimh,
> Trid na Trithinn ! trid na Triath !
> Comraig sinne, gleidh ar trial,
> Comraig sinne, gleidh ar trial.
>
> Athair ! A Mhic ! A Spioraid Naoimh !
> Bi 'eadh an Tri-Aon leinn, a la's a dh-oidhche !
> 'S air chul nan tonn, no air thaobh nam beann,
> Bi 'dh ar Mathair leinn, 's bith a lamh fo'r ceann,
> Bi 'dh ar Mathair leinn, 's bith a lamh fo'r ceann.

> Thou gentle Michael of the white steed,
> Who subdued the Dragon of blood,
> For love of God and the Son of Mary,
> Spread over us thy wing, shield us all !
> Spread over us thy wing, shield us all !
>
> Mary beloved ! Mother of the White Lamb,
> Protect us, thou Virgin of nobleness,
> Queen of beauty ! Shepherdess of the flocks !
> Keep our cattle, surround us together,
> Keep our cattle, surround us together.

---

[1] This hymn was taken down in the Gaelic and translated by Mr. Alexander Carmichael of South Uist.

Thou Colomba, the friendly, the kind,
In name of the Father, the Son, and the Spirit Holy,
Through the Three-in-One, through the Three,
Encompass us, guard our procession,
Encompass us, guard our procession.

Thou Father! thou Son! thou Spirit Holy!
Be the Three-in-One with us day and night.
And on the crested wave, or on the mountain-side,
Our Mother is there, and her arm is under our head,
Our Mother is there, and her arm is under our head.'

Alan found himself repeating whisperingly, and again and again—

'Bi 'eadh an Tri-Aon leinn, a la's a dh-oidhche!
'S air chul nan tonn, no air thaobh nam beann.'

Suddenly the woman glanced upward, perhaps because of the shadow that moved against the green bracken below. With a startled gesture she sprang to her feet. Alan looked at her kindly, saying, with a smile, 'Sure, Morag nic Tormod, it is not fear you need be having of one who is your friend.' Then, seeing that the woman stared at him with something of terror as well as surprise, he spoke to her again.

'Sure, Morag, I am no stranger that you should be looking at me with those foreign eyes.' He laughed as he spoke, and made as though he were about to descend to the burnside. Unmistakably, however, the woman did not desire his company. He saw this, with the pain and bewilderment which had come upon him whenever the like happened, as so often it had happened since he had come to Rona.

'Tell me, Morag MacNeill, what is the meaning of

this strangeness that is upon you? Why do you not speak? Why do you turn away your head?'

Suddenly the woman flashed her black eyes upon him.

'Have you ever heard of *am Buachaill Bàn—am Buachaill Buidhe*?'

He looked at her in amaze. *Am Buachaill Bàn!* ... The fair-haired Herdsman, the yellow-haired Herdsman! What could she mean? In days gone by, he knew, the islanders, in the evil time after Culloden, had so named the fugitive Prince who had sought shelter in the Hebrides; and in some of the runes of an older day still the Saviour of the World was sometimes so called, just as Mary was called *Bhuachaile nan treud*—Shepherdess of the Flock. But it could be no allusion to either of these that was intended.

'Who is the Herdsman of whom you speak, Morag?'

'Is it no knowledge you have of him at all, Alan MacAilean?'

'None. I know nothing of the man, nothing of what is in your mind. Who is the Herdsman?'

'You will not be putting evil upon me because that you saw me here by the pool before I saw you?'

'Why should I, woman? Why do you think that I have the power of the evil eye? Sure, I have done no harm to you or yours, and wish none. But if it is for peace to you to know it, it is no evil I wish you, but only good. The Blessing of Himself be upon you and yours and upon your house!'

The woman looked relieved, but still cast her furtive gaze upon Alan, who no longer attempted to join her.

'I cannot be speaking the thing that is in my mind, Alan MacAilean. It is not for me to be saying that thing. But if you have no knowledge of the Herdsman, sure it is only another wonder of the wonders, and God has the sun on that shadow, to the Stones be it said.'

'But tell me, Morag, who is the Herdsman of whom you speak?'

For a minute or more the woman stood regarding him intently. Then slowly, and with obvious reluctance, she spoke—

'Why have you appeared to the people upon the isle, sometimes by moonlight, sometimes by day or in the dusk, and have foretold upon one and all who dwell here black gloom and the red flame of sorrow? Why have you, who are an outcast because of what lies between you and another, pretended to be a messenger of the Son—ay, for sure, even, God forgive you, to be the Son Himself?'

Alan stared at the woman. For a time he could utter no word. Had some extraordinary delusion spread among the islanders, and was there in the insane accusation of this woman the secret of that which had so troubled him?

'This is all an empty darkness to me, Morag. Speak more plainly, woman. What is all this madness that you say? When have I spoken of having any mission, or of being other than I am? When have I foretold evil upon you or yours, or upon the isles beyond? What man has ever dared to say that Alan MacAilean of Rona is an outcast? And what sin is it that lies between me and another of which you know?'

It was impossible for Morag MacNeill to doubt the sincerity of the man who spoke to her. She crossed herself, and muttered the words of a *seun* for the protection of the soul against the demon powers. Still, even while she believed in Alan's sincerity, she could not reconcile it with that terrible and strange mystery with which rumour had filled her ears. So, having nothing to say in reply to his eager questions, she cast down her eyes and kept silence.

'Speak, Morag, for Heaven's sake! Speak if you are a true woman; you that see a man in sore pain, in pain, too, for that of which he knows nothing, and of the ill of which he is guiltless!'

But, keeping her face averted, the woman muttered simply, 'I have no more to say.' With that she turned and moved slowly along the pathway which led from the pool to her hillside bothie.

With a sigh, Alan walked slowly away. What wonder, he thought, that deep gloom had been upon him that day? Here, in the woman's mysterious words, was the shadow of that shadow.

Slowly, brooding deep over what he had heard, he crossed the Monadh-nan-Con, as the hill-tract there was called, till he came to the rocky wilderness known as the Slope of the Caverns.

There for a time he leaned against a high boulder, idly watching a few sheep nibbling the short grass which grew about some of the many caves which opened in slits or wide hollows. Below and beyond he saw the pale blue silence of the sea meet the pale blue silence of the sky; south-westward, the grey film of the coast of Ulster; westward, again the illimitable vast of sea and sky, infinitudes of calm, as though the blue silence of heaven breathed in that one motionless wave, as though that wave sighed and drew the horizons to its heart. From where he stood he could hear the murmur of the surge whispering all round the isle; the surge that, even on days of profound stillness, makes a murmurous rumour among the rocks and shingle of the island shores. Not upon the moor-side, but in the blank hollows of the caves around him, he heard, as in gigantic shells, the moving of a strange and solemn rhythm: wave-haunted shells indeed, for the echo that was bruited from one to the other came from beneath, from out of those labyrinthine passages and dim, shadowy sea-arcades, where among the melancholy green glooms the Atlantic waters lose themselves in a vain wandering.

For long he leaned there, revolving in his mind the mystery of Morag MacNeill's words. Then, abruptly, the stillness was broken by the sound of a dislodged stone. So little did he expect the foot of fellow-man, that he did not turn at what he thought to be the slip of a sheep. But when upon the slope of the grass, a little way beyond where he stood, a dusky blue shadow wavered fantastically, he swung round with a sudden instinct of dread.

And this was the dread which, after these long weeks since he had come to Rona, was upon Alan Carmichael.

For there, standing quietly by another boulder, at the mouth of another cave, was a man in all appearance identical with himself. Looking at this apparition, he beheld one of the same height as himself, with hair of the same hue, with eyes the same and features the same, with the same carriage, the same smile, the same expression. No, there, and there alone, was any difference.

Sick at heart, Alan wondered if he looked upon his own wraith. Familiar with the legends of his people, it would have been no strange thing to him that there, upon the hillside, should appear the wraith of himself. Had not old Ian MacIain—and that, too, though far away in a strange land—seen the death of his mother moving upward from her feet to her knees, from her knees to her waist, from her waist to her neck, and, just before the end, how the shroud darkened along the face until it hid the eyes? Had he not often heard from her, from Ian, of the second self which so often appears beside the living when already the shadow of doom is upon him whose hours are numbered? Was this, then, the reason of what had been his inexplicable gloom? Was he indeed at the extreme of life? Was his soul amid shallows, already a rock upon a blank, inhospitable shore? If not, who or what was this second self which leaned there negligently, looking at him with scornful smiling lips, but with intent, unsmiling eyes.

THE HERDSMAN

Slowly there came into his mind this thought: How could a phantom, that was itself intangible, throw a shadow upon the grass, as though it were a living body? Sure, a shadow there was indeed. It lay between the apparition and himself. A legend heard in boyhood came back to him; instinctively he stooped and lifted a stone and flung it midway into the shadow.

'Go back into the darkness,' he cried, 'if out of the darkness you came; but if you be a living thing, put out your hands!'

The shadow remained motionless. When Alan looked again at his second self, he saw that the scorn which had been upon the lips was now in the eyes also. Ay, for sure, scornful silent laughter it was that lay in those cold wells of light. No phantom that; a man he, even as Alan himself. His heart pulsed like that of a trapped bird, but with the spoken word his courage came back to him.

'Who are you?' he asked, in a voice strange even in his own ears.

'*Am Buachaill*,' replied the man in a voice as low and strange. 'I am the Herdsman.'

A new tide of fear surged in upon Alan. That voice, was it not his own? that tone, was it not familiar in his ears? When the man spoke, he heard himself speak; sure, if he were *Am Buachaill Bàn*, Alan, too, was the Herdsman, though what fantastic destiny might be his was all unknown to him.

'Come near,' said the man, and now the mocking

light in his eyes was wild as cloud-fire — 'come near, oh *Buachaill Bàn*!'

With a swift movement, Alan sprang forward; but as he leaped, his foot caught in a spray of heather, and he stumbled and fell. When he rose, he looked in vain for the man who had called him. There was not a sign, not a trace of any living being. For the first few moments he believed it had all been a delusion. Mortal being did not appear and vanish in that ghostly way. Still, surely he could not have mistaken the blank of that place for a speaking voice, nor out of nothingness have fashioned the living phantom of himself? Or could he? With that, he strode forward and peered into the wide arch of the cavern by which the man had stood. He could not see far into it; but so far as it was possible to see, he discerned neither man nor shadow of man, nor anything that stirred; no, not even the gossamer bloom of a beàrnan-brìde, that grew on a patch of grass a yard or two within the darkness, had lost one of its delicate filmy spires. He drew back, dismayed. Then, suddenly, his heart leaped again, for beyond all question, all possible doubt, there, in the bent thyme, just where the man had stood, was the imprint of his feet. Even now the green sprays were moving forward.

III

An hour passed, and Alan Carmichael had not moved from the entrance to the cave. So still was he that a ewe, listlessly wandering in search of cooler grass, lay down after a while, drowsily regarding him with her amber-coloured eyes. All his thought was upon the mystery of what he had seen. No delusion this, he was sure. That was a man whom he had seen. But who could he be? On so small an island, inhabited by less than a score of crofters, it was scarcely possible for one to live for many weeks and not know the name and face of every soul. Still, a stranger might have come. Only, if this were so, why should he call himself the Herdsman? There was but one herdsman on Rhona, and he Angus MacCormic, who lived at Einaval on the north side. In these outer isles, the shepherd and the herdsman are appointed by the community, and no man is allowed to be one or the other at will, any more than to be *maor*. Then, too, if this man were indeed herdsman, where was his *iomair-ionailtair*, his browsing tract? Looking round him, Alan could perceive nowhere any fitting pasture. Surely no herdsman would be content with such an *iomair a bhuachaill*—rig of the herdsman—as that rocky wilderness where the soft green grass grew in patches under this or that boulder, on the sun side of this or that rocky ledge. Again, he had given no name, but called himself simply *Am Buachaill*. This was how the woman Morag had spoken; did she indeed mean this very man? and if so, what lay in her words? But far beyond all other bewilderment for him was that strange, that indeed terrifying likeness to himself—a likeness so absolute, so convincing, that he knew he might himself easily have been deceived, had he

K

beheld the apparition in any place where it was possible that a reflection could have misled him.

Brooding thus, eye and ear were both alert for the faintest sight or sound. But from the interior of the cavern not a breath came. Once, from among the jagged rocks high on the west slope of Ben Einaval, he fancied he heard an unwonted sound—that of human laughter, but laughter so wild, so remote, so unmirthful, that fear was in his heart. It could not be other than imagination, he said to himself; for in that lonely place there was none to wander idly at that season, and none who, wandering, would laugh there solitary.

It was with an effort that Alan at last determined to probe the mystery. Stooping, he moved cautiously into the cavern, and groped his way along the narrow passage which led, as he thought, into another larger cave. But this proved to be one of the innumerable blind ways which intersect the honeycombed slopes of the Isle of Caves. To wander far in these lightless passages would be to track death. Long ago the piper whom the Prionnsa-Bàn, the Fair Prince, loved to hear in his exile—he that was called Rory M'Vurich—penetrated one of the larger hollows to seek there for a child that had idly wandered into the dark. Some of the clansmen, with the father and mother of the little one, waited at the entrance to the cave. For a time there was silence; then, as agreed upon, the sound of the pipes was heard, to which a man named Lachlan M'Lachlan replied from the outer air. The skirl of the pipes within grew fainter and fainter. Louder and louder Lachlan played upon his chanter; deeper and deeper grew the wild moaning of the drone; but for all that, fainter and fainter waned the sound of the pipes of Rory M'Vurich. Generations have come and gone upon the isle, and still no man has heard the returning air which Rory was to play. He may have found the little child, but he never found his backward path, and in the gloom of that honeycombed hill he and the child and the music of the pipes lapsed into the same stillness. Remembering this legend, familiar to him since his boyhood, Alan did not dare to venture further. At any moment, too, he knew he might fall into one of the crevices which opened into the sea-corridors hundreds of feet below. Ancient rumour had it that there were mysterious passages from the upper heights of Ben Einaval which led into the heart of this perilous maze. But for a time he lay still, straining every sense. Convinced at last that the man whom he sought had evaded all possible quest, he turned to regain the light. Brief way as he had gone, this was no easy thing to do. For a few moments, indeed, Alan lost his self-possession when he found a uniform dusk about him, and could not discern which of the several branching narrow corridors was that by which he had come. But following the greener light, he reached the cave, and soon, with a sigh of relief, was upon the sun-sweet warm earth again.

How more than ever beautiful the world seemed! how sweet to the eyes were upland and cliff, the wide stretch of ocean, the flying birds, the sheep grazing on the scanty pastures, and, above all, the homely blue smoke curling faintly upward from the fisher crofts on the headland east of Aonaig!

Purposely he retraced his steps by the way of the glen: he would see the woman Morag MacNeill again, and insist on some more explicit word. But when he reached the burnside once more, the woman was not there. Possibly she had seen him coming, and guessed his purpose; half he surmised this, for the peats in the hearth were brightly aglow, and on the hob beside them the boiling water hissed in a great iron pot wherein were potatoes. In vain he sought, in vain called. Impatient, he walked around the bothie and into the little byre beyond. The place was deserted. This, small matter as it was, added to his disquietude. Resolved to sift the mystery, he walked swiftly down the slope. By the old shealing of Cnoc-na-Monie, now forsaken, his heart leaped at sight of Ian coming to meet him.

When they met, Alan put his hands lovingly on the old man's shoulders, and looked at him with questioning eyes. He found rest and hope in those deep pools of quiet light, whence the faithful love rose comfortingly to meet his own yearning gaze.

'What is it, Alan-mo-ghray; what is the trouble that is upon you?'

'It is a trouble, Ian, but one of which I can speak little, for it is little I know.'

'Now, now, for sure you must tell me what it is.'

'I have seen a man here upon Rona whom I have

not seen or met before, and it is one whose face is known to me, and whose voice too, and one whom I would not meet again.'

'Did he give you no name?'

'None.'

'Where did he come from? Where did he go to?'

'He came out of the shadow, and into the shadow he went.'

Ian looked steadfastly at Alan, his wistful gaze searching deep into his unquiet eyes, and thence from feature to feature of the face which had become strangely worn of late.

But he questioned no further.

'I, too, Alan MacAilean, have heard a strange thing to-day. You know old Marsail Macrae? She is ill now with a slow fever, and she thinks that the shadow which she saw lying upon her hearth last Sabbath, when nothing was there to cause any shadow, was her own death, come for her, and now waiting there. I spoke to the old woman, but she would not have peace, and her eyes looked at me.

'"What will it be now, Marsail?" I asked.

'"Ay, ay, for sure," she said, "it was I who saw you first."

'"Saw me first, Marsail?"

'"Ay, you and Alan MacAilean."

'"When and where was this sight upon you?"

'"It was one month before you and he came to Rhona."

'I asked the poor old woman to be telling me her meaning. At first I could make little of what was said, for she muttered low, an' moved her head this way and that, an' moaned like a stricken ewe. But on my taking her hand, she looked at me again, and then told me this thing—

'"On the seventh day of the month before you came—and by the same token it was on the seventh day of the month following that you and Alan MacAilean came to Caisteal-Rhona—I was upon the shore at Aonaig, listening to the crying of the wind against the great cliff of Biola-creag. With me were Ruaridh Macrae and Neil MacNeill, Morag MacNeill, and her sister Elsa; and we were singing the hymn for those who were out on the wild sea that was roaring white against the cliffs of Berneray, for some of our people were there, and we feared for them. Sometimes one sang, and sometimes another. And, sure, it is remembering I am, how, when I had called out with my old wailing voice—

'"Bi 'eadh an Tri-aon leinn, a la's a dh-oidche;
'S air chul nan tonn, A Mhoire ghradhach!

(Be the Three-in-One with us day and night;
And on the crested wave, O Mary Belovëd!)

'"Now when I had just sung this, and we were all listening to the sound of it caught by the wind and blown up against the black face of Biola-creag, I saw a boat come sailing into the haven. I called out to those about me, but they looked at me with white faces, for no boat was there, and it was a rough, wild sea it was in that haven.

'"And in that boat I saw three people sitting; and one was you, Ian MacIain, and one was Alan MacAilean, and one was a man who had his face in shadow, and his eyes looked into the shadow at his feet. I saw you clear, and told those about me what I saw. And Seumas MacNeill, him that is dead now, and brother to Neil here at Aonaig, he said to me, 'Who was that whom you saw walking in the dusk the night before last?'—'Ailean MacAlasdair Carmichael,' answered one at that. Seumas muttered, looking at those about him, 'Mark what I say, for it is a true thing—that Ailean Carmichael of Rhona is dead now, because Marsail saw him walking in the dusk when he was not upon the island; and now, you Neil, and you Rory, and all of you, will be for thinking with me that one of the men in the boat whom Marsail sees now will be the son of him who has changed.'

'"Well, well, it is a true thing that we each of us thought that thought, but when the days went and nothing more came of it, the memory of the seeing went too. Then there came the day when the coble of Aulay MacAulay came out of Borosay into Caisteal-Rhona haven. Glad we were to see your face again, Ian MacIain, and to hear the sob of joy coming out of the heart of Giorsal your sister; but when you and Alan MacAilean came on shore, it was my voice that then went from mouth to mouth, for I whispered to Morag MacNeill who was next me that you were the men I had seen in the boat."

'Well, after that,' Ian added, with a grave smile, 'I spoke gently to old Marsail, and told her that there was no evil in that seeing, and that for sure it was nothing at all, at all, to see two people in a boat, and nothing coming of that, save happiness for those two, and glad content to be here.

'Marsail looked at me with big eyes.

'But when I asked her what she meant by that, she would say no more. No asking of mine would bring the word to her lips, only she shook her head and kept her gaze from my face. Then, seeing that it was useless, I said to her—

'"Marsail, tell me this: Was this sight of yours the sole thing that made the people here on Rona look askance at Alan MacAilean?"

'For a time she stared at me with dim eyes, then suddenly she spoke—

'"It is not all."

'"Then what more is there, Marsail Macrae?"

'"That is not for the saying. I have no more to say. Let you, or Alan MacAilean, go elsewhere. That which is to be, will be. To each his own end."

'"Then be telling me this now at least," I asked: " is there danger for him or me in this island?"

'But the poor old woman would say no more, and then I saw a swoon was on her.'

After this, Alan and Ian walked slowly home together, both silent, and each revolving in his mind as in a dim dusk that mystery which, vague and unreal at first, had now become a living presence, and haunted them by day and night.

IV

'In the shadow of pain, one may hear the footsteps of joy.' So runs a proverb of old.

It was a true saying for Alan. That night he lay down in pain, his heart heavy with the weight of a mysterious burden. On the morrow he woke blithely to a new day—a day of absolute beauty. The whole wide wilderness of ocean was of living azure, aflame with gold and silver. Around the promontories of the isles the brown-sailed fishing-boats of Barra and Berneray, of Borosay and Seila, moved blithely hither and thither. Everywhere the rhythm of life pulsed swift and strong. The first sound which had awakened Alan was of a loud singing of fishermen who were putting out from Aonaig. The coming of a great shoal of mackerel had been signalled, and every man and woman of the near isles was alert for the take. The watchers had known it by the swift congregation of birds, particularly the gannets and skuas. And as the men pulled at the oars, or hoisted the brown sails, they sang a snatch of an old-world tune, still chanted at the first coming of the birds when spring-tide is on the flow again—

> 'Bui' cheas dha 'n Ti thaine na Gugachan
> Thaine's na h-Eoin-Mhora cuideriu,
> Cailin dugh ciaru bo's a chro !
> Bo dhonn ! bo dhonn ! bo dhonn bheadarrach !
> Bo dhonn a ruin a bhlitheadh am baine dhuit
> Ho ro ! mo gheallag ! ni gu rodagach !
> Cailin dugh ciaru bo's a chro—
> Na h-eoin air tighinn ! cluinneam an ceol !'

(Thanks to the Being, the Gannets have come,
Yes! and the Great Auks along with them.
Dark-haired girl!—a cow in the fold!
Brown cow! brown cow! brown cow, beloved ho!
Brown cow! my love! the milker of milk to thee!
Ho ro! my fair-skinned girl—a cow in the fold,
And the birds have come!—glad sight, I see!)

Eager to be of help, Ian put off in his boat, and was soon among the fishermen, who in their new excitement were forgetful of all else than that the mackerel were come, and that every moment was precious. For the first time Ian found himself no unwelcome comrade. Was it, he wondered, because that, there upon the sea, whatever of shadow dwelled about him, or rather about Alan MacAilean, on the land, was no longer visible.

All through that golden noon he and the others worked hard. From isle to isle went the chorus of the splashing oars and splashing nets; of the splashing of the fish and the splashing of gannets and gulls; of the splashing of the tide leaping blithely against the sun-dazzle, and the illimitable rippling splash moving out of the west;—all this blent with the loud, joyous cries, the laughter, and the hoarse shouts of the men of Barra and the adjacent islands. It was close upon dusk before the Rhona boats put into the haven of Aonaig again; and by that time none was blither than Ian MacIain, who in that day of happy toil had lost all the gloom and apprehension of the day before, and now returned to Caisteal-Rhona with lighter heart than he had known for long.

When, however, he got there, there was no sign of Alan. He had gone, said Giorsal, he had gone out in the smaller boat midway in the afternoon, and had sailed around to Aoidhu, the great scaur which ran out beyond the precipices at the south-west of Rhona.

This Alan often did, and of late more and more often. Ever since he had come to the Hebrid Isles his love of the sea had deepened, and had grown into a passion for its mystery and beauty. Of late, too, something impelled to a more frequent isolation, a deep longing to be where no eye could see and no ear hearken.

So at first Ian was in no way alarmed. But when the sun had set, and over the faint blue film of the Isle of Tiree the moon had risen, and still no sign of Alan, he became restless and uneasy. Giorsal begged him in vain to eat of the supper she had prepared. Idly he moved to and fro along the rocky ledge, or down by the pebbly shore, or across the green *àiridh*, eager for a glimpse of him whom he loved so well.

At last, unable longer to endure a growing anxiety, he put out in his boat, and sailed swiftly before the slight easterly breeze which had prevailed since moonrise. So far as Aoidhu, all the way from Aonaig, there was not a haven anywhere, nor even one of the sea caverns which honeycombed the isle beyond the headland. A glance, therefore, showed him that Alan had not yet come back that way. It was possible, though unlikely, that he had sailed right round Rona; unlikely, because in the narrow straits to the north, between Rona and the scattered islets known as the Innsemhara, strong currents prevailed, and particularly at the full of the tide, when they swept north-eastward dark and swift as a mill-race.

Once the headland was passed and the sheer precipitous westward cliffs loomed black out of the sea, he became more and more uneasy. As yet, there was no danger; but he saw that a swell was moving out of the west; and whenever the wind blew that way, the sea arcades were filled with a lifting, perilous wave. Later, escape might be difficult, and often impossible. Out of the score or more great passages which opened between Aoidhu and Ardgorm, it was difficult to know into which to chance the search of Alan. Together they had examined all of them. Some twisted but slightly; others wound sinuously till the green, serpentine alleys, flanked by basalt walls hundreds of feet high, lost themselves in an indistinguishable maze.

But that which was safest, and wherein a boat could most easily make its way against wind or tide, was the huge, cavernous passage known locally as the Uaimh-nan-roin, the Cave of the Seals.

For this opening Ian steered his boat. Soon he was within the wide corridor. Like the great cave at Staffa, it was wrought as an aisle in some natural cathedral; the rocks, too, were columnar, and rose in flawless symmetry, as though graven by the hand of man. At the far end of this gigantic aisle, there diverges a long, narrow arcade, filled by day with the green shine of the water, and by night, when the moon is up, with a pale froth of light. It is one of the few where there are open gateways for the sea and the wandering light, and by its spherical shape almost the only safe passage in a season of heavy wind. Half-way along this arched arcade a corridor leads to a round cup-like cavern, midway in which stands a huge mass of black basalt, in shape suggestive of a titanic altar. Thus it must have impressed the imagination of the islanders of old; for by them, even in a remote day, it was called Teampull-Mara, the Temple of the Sea. Owing to the narrowness of the passage, and to the smooth, unbroken walls which rise sheer from the green depths into an invisible darkness, the Strait of the Temple is not one wherein to linger long, save in a time of calm.

Instinctively, however, Ian quietly headed his boat along this narrow way. When, silently, he emerged from the arcade, he could just discern the mass of basalt at the far end of the cavern. But there, seated in his boat, was Alan, apparently idly adrift, for one oar floated in the water alongside, and the other swung listlessly from the tholes.

His heart had a suffocating grip as he saw him whom he had come to seek. Why that absolute stillness, that strange, listless indifference? For a dreadful moment he feared death had indeed come to him in that lonely place where, as an ancient legend had it, a woman of old time had perished, and ever since had wrought death upon any who came thither solitary and unhappy.

But at the striking of the shaft of his oar against a ledge, Alan moved, and looked at him with startled eyes. Half rising from where he crouched in the stern, he called to him in a voice that had in it something strangely unfamiliar.

'I will not hear!' he cried. 'I will not hear! Leave me! Leave me!'

Fearing that the desolation of the place had wrought upon his mind, Ian swiftly moved toward him, and the next moment his boat glided alongside. Stepping from the one to the other, he kneeled beside him.

'*Ailean mo caraid, Ailean-aghray*, what is it? What gives you dread? There is no harm here. All is well. Look! See, it is I, Ian—old Ian MacIain! Listen, *mo ghaoil*; do you not know me—do you not know who I am? It is I, Ian; Ian who loves you!'

Even in that obscure light he could clearly discern the pale face, and his heart smote him as he saw Alan's eyes turn upon him with a glance wild and mournful. Had he indeed succumbed to the sea madness which ever and again strikes into a terrible melancholy one here and there among those who dwell in the remote isles? But even as he looked, he noted another expression come into the wild strained eyes; and almost before he realised what had happened, Alan was on his feet and pointing with rigid arm.

For there, in that nigh unreachable and for ever unvisited solitude, was the figure of a man. He stood on the summit of the huge basalt altar, and appeared to have sprung from out the rock, or, himself a shadowy presence, to have grown out of the obscure unrealities of the darkness. Ian stared, fascinated, speechless.

Then with a spring he was on the ledge. Swift and sure as a wild cat, he scaled the huge mass of the altar.

Nothing; no one! There was not a trace of any human being. Not a bird, not a bat; nothing. Moreover, even in that slowly blackening darkness, he could see that there was no direct connection between the summit or side with the blank, precipitous wall of basalt beyond. Overhead there was, so far as he could discern, a vault. No human being could have descended through that perilous gulf.

Was the island haunted? he wondered, as slowly he made his way back to the boat. Or had he been startled into some wild fantasy, and imagined a likeness where none had been? Perhaps even he had not really seen any one. He had heard of such things. The nerves can soon chase the mind into the shadow wherein it loses itself.

Or was Alan the vain dreamer? That, indeed, might well be. Mayhap he had heard some fantastic tale from Morag MacNeill, or from old Marsail Macrae; the islanders had *sgeul* after *sgeul* of a wild strangeness.

In silence he guided the boats back into the outer arcade, where a faint sheen of moonlight glistered on the water. Thence, in a few minutes, he oared that wherein he and Alan sat, with the other fastened astern, into the open.

When the moonshine lay full on Alan's face, Ian saw that he was thinking neither of himself nor of where he was. His eyes were heavy with dream.

What wind there was blew against their course, so Ian rowed unceasingly. In silence they passed once again the headland of Aoidhu; in silence they drifted past a single light gleaming in a croft near Aonaig—a red eye staring out into the shadow of the sea, from the room where the woman Marsail lay dying; and in silence their keels grided on the patch of shingle in Caisteal-Rhona haven.

For days thereafter Alan haunted that rocky, cavernous wilderness where he had seen the Herdsman.

It was in vain he had sought everywhere for some tidings of this mysterious dweller in those upland solitudes. At times he believed that there was indeed some one upon the island of whom, for inexplicable reasons, none there would speak; but at last he came to the conviction that what he had seen was an apparition, projected by the fantasy of overwrought nerves. Even from the woman Morag MacNeill, to whom he had gone with a frank appeal that won its way to her heart, he learned no more than that an old legend, of which she did not care to speak, was in some way associated with his own coming to Rona.

Ian, too, never once alluded to the mysterious

incident of the green arcades which had so deeply impressed them both: never after Alan had told him that he had seen a vision.

But as the days passed, and as no word came to either of any unknown person who was on the island, and as Alan, for all his patient wandering and furtive quest, both among the upland caves and in the green arcades, found absolutely no traces of him whom he sought, the belief that he had been duped by his imagination deepened almost to conviction.

As for Ian, he, unlike Alan, became more and more convinced that what he had seen was indeed no apparition. Whatever lingering doubt he had was dissipated on the eve of the night when old Marsail Macrae died. It was dusk when word came to Caisteal-Rhona that Marsail felt the cold wind on the soles of her feet. Ian went to her at once, and it was in the dark hour which followed that he heard once more, and more fully, the strange story which, like a poisonous weed, had taken root in the minds of the islanders. Already from Marsail he had heard of the Prophet, though, strangely enough, he had never breathed word of this to Alan, not even when, after the startling episode of the apparition in the Teampull-Mara, he had, as he believed, seen the Prophet himself. But there in the darkness of the low, turfed cottage, with no light in the room save the dull red gloom from the heart of the smoored peats, Marsail, in the attenuated, remote voice of those who have already entered into the vale of the shadow, told him this thing, in the homelier Gaelic—

'Yes, Ian mac Iain-Bàn, I will be telling you this thing before I change. You are for knowing, sure, that long ago Uilleam, brother of him who was father to the lad up at the castle yonder, had a son? Yes, you know that, you say, and also that he was called Donnacha Bàn? No, mo-caraid, that is not a true thing that you have heard, that Donnacha Bàn went under the wave years ago. He was the seventh son, and was born under the full moon; 'tis Himself will be knowing whether that was for or against him. Of these seven none lived beyond childhood except the two youngest, Kenneth and Donnacha. Kenneth was always frail as a February flower, but he lived to be a man. He and his brother never spoke, for a feud was between them, not only because that each was unlike the other, and the younger hated the older because thus he was the penniless one, but most because both loved the same woman. I am not for telling you the whole story now, for the breath in my body will soon blow out in the draught that is coming upon me; but this I will say to you: darker and darker grew the gloom between these brothers. When Giorsal Macdonald gave her love to Kenneth, Donnacha disappeared for a time. Then, one day, he came back to Borosay, and smiled quietly with his cold eyes when they wondered at his coming again. Now, too, it was noticed that he no longer had an ill-will upon his brother, but spoke smoothly with him and loved to be in his company. But to this day no one knows for sure what happened. For there was a gloaming when Donnacha Bàn came back alone in his sailing-boat. He and Kenneth had sailed forth, he said, to shoot seals in the sea-arcades to the west of Rona, but in these dark and lonely passages they had missed each other. At last he had heard Kenneth's voice calling for help, but when he had got to the place it was too late, for his brother had been seized with the cramps, and had sunk deep into the fathomless water. There is no getting a body again that sinks in these sea-galleries. The crabs know that.

'Well, this and much more was what Donnacha Bàn told to his people. None believed him; but what could any do? There was no proof; none had ever seen them enter the sea-caves together. Not that Donnacha Bàn sought in any way to keep back those who would fain know more. Not so; he strove to help to find the body. Nevertheless, none believed; and Giorsal nic Dugall Mòr least of all. The blight of that sorrow went to her heart. She had death soon, poor thing! but before the cold greyness was upon her she told her father, and the minister that was there, that she knew Donnacha Bàn had murdered his brother. One might be saying these were the wild words of a woman; but, for sure, no one said that thing upon Borosay or Rona, or any of these isles. When all was done, the minister told what he knew, and what he thought, to the Lord of the South Isles, and asked what was to be put upon Donnacha Bàn. "Exile for ever," said the chief, "or if he stays here, the doom of silence. Let no man or woman speak to him or give him food or drink, or give him shelter, or let his shadow cross his or hers."

'When this thing was told to Donnacha Bàn Carmichael, he laughed at first; but as day after day slid over the rocks where all days fall, he laughed no more. Soon he saw that the chief's word was no empty word; and yet he would not go away from his own place. He could not stay upon Borosay, for his father cursed him; and no man can stay upon the island where a father's curse moves this way and that, for ever seeking him. Then, some say a madness came upon him, and others that he took wildness to be his way, and others that God put upon him the shadow of loneliness, so that he might meet sorrow there and repent. Howsoever that may be, Donnacha Bàn came to Rona, and, by the same token, it was the year of the great blight, when the potatoes and the corn came to naught, and when the fish in the sea swam away from the isles. In the autumn of that year there was not a soul left on Rona except Giorsal and the old man Ian, her father, who had guard of Caisteal-Rhona for him who was absent. When, once more, years after, smoke rose from the crofts, the saying spread that Donnacha Bàn, the murderer, had made his home among the caves of the upper part of the isle. None knew how this saying rose, for he was seen of none. The last man who saw him—and that was a year later—was old Padruic M'Vurich the shepherd. Padruic said that, as he was driving his ewes across the north slope of Ben Einaval in the gloaming, he came upon a silent figure seated upon a rock, with his chin in his hands, and his elbows on his knees—with the great, sad eyes of him staring at the moon that was lifting itself out of the sea. Padruic did not know who the man was. The shepherd had few wits, poor man! and he had known, or remembered, little about the story of Donnacha Bàn Carmichael; so when he spoke to the man, it was as to a stranger. The man looked at him and said—

'" You are Padruic M'Vurich, the shepherd."

'At that a trembling was upon old Padruic, who had the wonder that this stranger should know who and what he was.

'" And who will you be, and forgive the saying?" he asked.

'" *Am Fàidh*—the Prophet," the man said.

'" And what prophet will you be, and what is your prophecy?" asked Padruic.

'" I am here because I wait for what is to be, and that will be the coming of the Woman who is the Daughter of God."

'And with that the man said no more, and the old shepherd went down through the gloaming, and, heavy with the thoughts that troubled him, followed his ewes down into Aonaig. But after that neither he nor any other saw or heard tell of the shadowy stranger; so that all upon Rona felt sure that Padruic had beheld no more than a vision. There were some who thought that he had seen the ghost of the outlaw Donnacha Bàn; and mayhap one or two who wondered if the stranger that had said he was a prophet was not Donnacha Bàn himself, with a madness come upon him; but at last these sayings went out to sea upon the wind, and men forgot. But, and it was months and months afterwards, and three days before his own death, old Padruic M'Vurich was sitting in the sunset on the rocky ledge in front of his brother's croft, where then he was staying, when he heard a strange crying of seals. He thought little of that; only, when he looked closer, he saw, in the hollow of the wave hard by that ledge, a drifting body.

'"*Am Fàidh — Am Fàidh!*" he cried; "the Prophet, the Prophet!"

' At that his brother and his brother's wife ran to see; but it was nothing that they saw. "It would be a seal," said Pòl M'Vurich; but at that Padruic had shook his head, and said no for sure, he had seen the face of the dead man, and it was of him whom he had met on the hillside, and that had said he was the Prophet who was waiting there for the second coming of God.

' And that is how there came about the echo of the thought that Donnacha Bàn had at last, after his madness, gone under the green wave and was dead. For all that, in the months which followed, more than one man said he had seen a figure high up on the hill. The old wisdom says that when God comes again, or the prophet who will come before, it will be as a herdsman on a lonely isle. More than one of the old people on Rona and Borosay remembered that *sgeul* out of the *Seanachas* that the tale-tellers knew. There were some who said that Donnacha Bàn had never been drowned at all, and that he was this Prophet, this Herdsman. Others would not have that saying at all, but believed that the wraith was indeed Am Buachaill Bàn, the Fair-haired Shepherd, who had come again to redeem the people out of their sorrow. There were even those who said that the Herdsman who haunted Rona was no other than Kenneth Carmichael himself, who had not died but had had the mind-dark there in the sea-caves where he had been lost, and there had come to the knowledge of secret things, and so was at last Am Fàidh Chriosd.'

A great weakness came upon the old woman when she had spoken thus far. Ian feared that she would have breath for no further word; but after a thin gasping, and a listless fluttering of weak hands upon the coverlet, whereon her trembling fingers plucked aimlessly at the invisible blossoms of death, she opened her eyes once more, and stared in a dim questioning at him who sat by her bedside.

'Tell me,' whispered Ian, 'tell me, Marsail, what thought it is that is in your own mind?'

But already the old woman had begun to wander.

'For sure, for sure,' she muttered, '*Am Fàidh* . . . *Am Fàidh* . . . an' a child will be born . . . the Queen of Heaven, an' . . . that will be the voice of Domhuill, my husband, I am hearing . . . an' dark it is, an' the tide comin' in . . . an'——'

Then, sure, the tide came in, and if in that darkness old Marsail Macrae heard any voice at all, it was that of Domhuill who years agone had sunk into the wild seas off the head of Barra.

An hour later Alan walked slowly under the cloudy night. All he had heard from Ian came back to him with a strange familiarity. Something of this, at least, he had known before. Some hints of this mysterious Herdsman had reached his ears. In some inexplicable way his real or imaginary presence there upon Rona seemed a pre-ordained thing for him.

He knew that the wild imaginings of the islanders had woven the legend of the Prophet, or of his mysterious message, out of the loom of the deep longing whereon is woven that larger tapestry, the shadow-thridden life of the island Gael. Laughter and tears, ordinary hopes and pleasures, and even joy itself, and bright gaiety, and the swift spontaneous imaginations of susceptible natures—all this, of course, is to be found with the island Gael as with his fellows elsewhere. But every here and there are some who have in their minds the inheritance from the dim past of their race, and are oppressed as no other people are oppressed by the gloom of a strife between spiritual emotion and material facts. It is the brains of dreamers such as these which clear the mental life of the community; and it is in these brains are the mysterious looms which weave the tragic and sorrowful tapestries of Celtic thought. It were a madness to suppose that life in the isles consists of nothing but sadness or melancholy. It is not so, or need not be so, for the Gael is a creature of shadow and shine. But whatever the people is, the brain of the Gael hears a music that is sadder than any music there is, and has for its cloudy sky a gloom that shall not go; for the end is near, and upon the westernmost shores of these remote isles the voice of Celtic sorrow may be heard crying, '*Cha till, cha till, cha till mi tuille*': 'I will return, I will return, I will return no more.'

Alan knew all this well; and yet he too dreamed his dream—that, even yet, there might be redemption for the people. He did not share the wild hope which some of the older islanders held, that Christ Himself shall come again to redeem an oppressed race; but might not another saviour arise, another redeeming spirit come into the world? And if so, might not that child of joy be born out of suffering and sorrow and crime; and if so, might not the Herdsman be indeed a prophet, the Prophet of the Woman in whom God should come anew as foretold?

With startled eyes he crossed the thyme-set ledge whereon stood Caisteal-Rhona. Was it, after all, a message he had received, and was that which had appeared to him in that lonely cavern of the sea but a phantom of his own destiny? Was he himself, Alan Carmichael, indeed *Am Fàidh*, the predestined Prophet of the isles?

V

Ever since the night of Marsail's death, Ian had noticed that Alan no longer doubted, but that in some way a special message had come to him, a special revelation. On the other hand, he had himself swung further into his conviction that the vision he had seen in the cavern was, in truth, that of a living man. On Borosay, he knew, the fishermen believed that the *aonaran nan creag*, the recluse of the rocks, as commonly they spoke of him, was no other than Donnacha Bàn Carmichael, survived there through these many years, and long since mad with his loneliness and because of the burden of his crime.

But by this time the islanders had come to see that Alan MacAilean was certainly not Donnacha Bàn. Even the startling likeness no longer betrayed them in this way. The ministers and the priests on Berneray and Barra scoffed at the whole story, and everywhere discouraged the idea that Donnacha Bàn could still be among the living. But for the common belief that to encounter the Herdsman, whether the lost soul of Donnacha Bàn or indeed the strange phantom of the hills of which the old legends spoke, was to meet inevitable disaster, the islanders might have been persuaded to make such a search among the caves of Rona as would almost certainly have revealed the presence of any who dwelt therein.

But as summer lapsed into autumn, and autumn

itself through its golden silences waned into the shadow of the equinox, a strange, brooding serenity came upon Alan. Ian himself now doubted his own vision of the mysterious Herdsman—if he indeed existed at all except in the imaginations of those who spoke of him either as the Buachaill Bàn, or as the *aonaran nan creag*. If a real man, Ian believed that at last he had passed away. None saw the Herdsman now; and even Morag MacNeill, who had often on moonlight nights been startled by the sound of a voice chanting among the upper solitudes, admitted that she now heard nothing unusual.

St. Martin's summer came at last, and with it all that wonderful, dreamlike beauty which bathes the isles in a flood of golden light, and draws over sea and land a veil of deeper mystery.

One late afternoon, Ian, returning to Caisteal-Rhona after an unexplained absence of several hours, found Alan sitting at a table. Spread before him were the sheets of one of the strange old Gaelic tales which he had ardently begun to translate. Alan lifted and slowly read the page of paraphrase which he had just laid down. It was after the homelier Gaelic of the *Eachdaireachd Challum mhic Cruimein*.

'And when that king had come to the island, he lived there in the shadow of men's eyes; for none saw him by day or by night, and none knew whence he came or whither he fared; for his feet were shod with silence, and his way with dusk. But men knew that he was there, and all feared him. Months, even years, tramped one on the heels of the other, and perhaps the king gave no sign, but one day he would give a sign; and that sign was a laughing that was heard somewhere, upon the lonely hills, or on the lonely wave, or in the heart of him who heard. And whenever the king laughed, he who heard would fare ere long from his fellows to join that king in the shadow. But sometimes the king laughed only because of vain hopes and wild imaginings, for upon these he lives as well as upon the strange savours of mortality.'

That night Alan awakened Ian suddenly, and taking him by the hand made him promise to go with him on the morrow to the Teampull-Mara.

In vain Ian questioned him as to why he asked this thing. All Alan would say was that he must go there once again, and with him, for he believed that a spirit out of heaven had come to reveal to him a wonder. Distressed by what he knew to be a madness, and fearful that it might prove to be no passing fantasy, Ian would fain have persuaded him against this intention. Even as he spoke, however, he realised that it might be better to accede to his wishes, and, above all, to be there with him, so that it might not be one only who heard or saw the expected revelation.

And it was a strange faring indeed, that which occurred on the morrow. At noon, when the tide was an hour turned in the ebb, they sailed westward from Caisteal-Rhona. It was in silence they made that strange journey together; for, while Ian steered, Alan lay down in the hollow of the boat, with his head against the old man's knees, and slept, or at least lay still with his eyes closed.

When at last they passed the headland and entered the first of the sea-arcades, Alan rose and sat beside him. Hauling down the now useless sail, Ian took an oar and, standing at the prow, urged the boat inward along the narrow corridor which led to the huge sea-cave of the Altar.

In the deep gloom—for even on that day of golden light and beauty the green air of the sea-cave was heavy with shadow—there was a deathly chill. What dull light there was came from the sheen of the green water which lay motionless along the black basaltic ledges. When at last the base of the Altar was reached, Ian secured the boat by a rope passed around a projecting spur, and then seated himself in the stern beside Alan.

'Tell me, Alan-a-ghaoil, what is this thing that you are thinking you will hear or see?'

Alan looked at him strangely for a while, but, though his lips moved, he said nothing.

'Tell me, my heart,' Ian urged again, 'who is it you expect to see or hear?'

'*Am Buachaill Bàn*,' Alan answered, 'the Herdsman.'

For a moment Ian hesitated. Then, taking Alan's hand in his and raising it to his lips, he whispered in his ear—

'There is no Herdsman upon Rona. If a man was there who lived solitary, the *aonaran nan creag* is dead long since. What you have seen and heard has been a preying upon you of wild thoughts. Be thinking no more now of this vision.'

'This man,' Alan answered quietly, 'is not Donnacha Bàn, but the Prophet of whom the people speak. He himself has told me this thing. Yesterday I was here, and he bade me come again. He spoke out of the shadow that is about the Altar, though I saw him not. I asked him if he were Donnacha Bàn, and he said "No." I asked him if he were *Am Fàidh*, and he said "Yes." I asked him if he were indeed an immortal spirit and herald of that which was to be, and he said "Even so."'

For a long while after this no word was spoken. The chill of that remote place began to affect Alan, and he shivered slightly at times. But more he shivered because of the silence, and because that he who had promised to be there gave no sign. Sure, he thought, it could not be all a dream; sure, the Herdsman would come again.

Then at last, turning to Ian, he said, 'We must come on the morrow, for to-day he is not here.'

'I will do what you ask, Alan-mo-ghaol.'

But of a sudden Alan stepped on the black ledges at the base of the Altar, and slowly mounted the precipitous rock.

Ian watched him till he became a shadow in that darkness. His heart leaped when suddenly he heard a cry fall out of the gloom.

'Alan, Alan!' he cried, and a great fear was upon him when no answer came; but at last he heard him clambering slowly down the perilous slope of that obscure place. When he reached the ledge Alan stood still regarding him.

'Why do you not come into the boat?' Ian asked, terrified because of what he saw in Alan's eyes.

Alan looked at him with parted lips, his breath coming and going like that of a caged bird.

'What is it?' Ian whispered.

'Ian, when I reached the top of the Altar, and in the dim light that was there, I saw the dead body of a man lying upon the rock. His head was lain back so that the gleam from a crevice in the cliff overhead fell upon it. The man has been dead many hours. He is a man whose hair has been greyed by years and sorrow, but the man is he who is of my blood; he whom I resemble so closely; he that the fishermen call the hermit of the rocks; he that is the Herdsman.'

Ian stared, with moving lips: then in a whisper he spoke—

'Would you be for following a herdsman who could lead you to no fold? This man is dead, Alan mac Alasdair; and it is well that you brought me here to-day. That is a good thing, and for sure God has willed it.'

'It is not a man that is dead. It is my soul that lies there. It is dead. God called me to be His Prophet, and I hid in dreams. It is the end.' And with that, and death staring out of his eyes, he entered the boat and sat down beside Ian.

'Let us go,' he said, and that was all.

Slowly Ian oared the boat across the shadowy

gulf of the cave, along the narrow passage, and into the pale green gloom of the outer cavern, wherein the sound of the sea made a forlorn requiem in his ears.

But the short November day was already passing to its end. All the sea westward was aflame with gold and crimson light, and in the great dome of the sky a wonderful radiance lifted above the paleness of the clouds, whose pinnacled and bastioned heights towered in the south-west.

A faint wind blew eastwardly. Raising the sail, Ian made it fast and then sat down beside Alan. But he, rising, moved along the boat to the mast, and leaned there with his face against the setting sun.

Idly they drifted onward. Deep silence lay between them; deep silence was all about them, save for the ceaseless, inarticulate murmur of the sea, the splash of low waves against the rocks of Rona, and the sigh of the surf at the base of the basalt precipices.

And this was their homeward sailing on that day of revelation: Alan, with his back against the mast, and his lifeless face irradiated by the light of the setting sun; Ian, steering, with his face in shadow.

II

M

'*I have tried to feed myself on hopes and dreams
all through these years.*'
                    JOHN GABRIEL BORKMAN.

'*Come to me in my dreams, and then
By day I shall be well again!
For so the night will more than pay
The hopeless longing of the day.*'

'*Some there are who do thus in beauty love
each other.*'
          MAETERLINCK: La Beauté Intérieure.

THE BOOK OF THE OPAL

WHEN my kinsman Ambrose Stuart died last year, he left me many papers, family documents, and the MS. of a book, the third and final part of it unfinished. He died, where for some years he had lived, in Venice. I remember when he went: it was to join his intimate friend and foster-brother, Carolan Stuart, spiritual head of a House of Rest there: and he left his birth-isle in the Hebrides because he could no longer be a priest, having found a wisdom older than that he professed, and gods more ancient than his own, and a vision of august beauty, that was not greater than that which dreaming souls see through the incense of the Church—because there is no greater or lesser beauty in the domain of the spirit, but only Beauty—but was to him higher in its heights and deeper in its depths.

The first part of this book is his own story, from childhood to manhood : a story of a remote life, remotely lived; of a singular and pathetic loneliness. The second deals with his thoughts and dreams in Rome during his novitiate, his life in Paris, his priesthood in the Southern Hebrides. The third, and much the longest, though unfinished, is less a narrative than a journal, and begins from the day when he first knew that the prayers in his mind shaped themselves otherwise than as they came to his lips; and that ~~old~~ forgotten wisdom of his people came nearer to his spirit than many sacred words, which, to him, were not the wind, but the infinite circling maze of leaves blown before the wind.

The papers were, for the most part, pages written during those dull days of idle or perplexed thought which came between this change and his abrupt relinquishing of the priesthood. ~~They are not pleasant to me.~~ A bitter spirit inhabits them: a spirit of the flesh, and the things of the flesh, and of the dust. Among the latest are one or two of which I am glad, for they show that he sought evil, or if not evil, the common ways of evil, as a man will take a poison to avert death.

The third part of the book comes to within a few days of his death. It deals with his life in Venice: with his inner life, for he lived solitary, and went little among his fellows, and for the most part dwelled with Father Carolan at the Casa San Spirito in the Rio del Occidente.

It was there I saw him a week before his death. I was in Italy, where I had gone for a light and warm air, after a northern winter damp and bleak beyond any I have known: and when I had a letter from him, begging me to leave my friends and to come to Venice to see him before death put him beyond these too many dreams, I went.

From these papers, from that unfinished book, I learned much of a singular and perplexing nature.

I believe more readily now that a man or woman may be possessed: or, that two spirits may inhabit the same body, as fire and air together inhabit a jet of flame.

'I am shaken with desire,' he writes in one place, 'and not any wind can blow that fire out of my heart. There is no room for even one little flaming word of God in my heart. When I am not shaken with desires, it is only because I am become Desire. And my desire is all evil. It is not of the mind or of the body only, but is of the mind and the body and the spirit. It is my pleasure to deny God. I have no fear. Sweet, intolerable lust possesses me.'

And yet, within a page or two of where these words are, and written later on the same day, I find: 'There is a star within me which guides me through all darkness. Pride is evil, but there is a pride which great angels know, they who do not stoop, who hear but do not listen. What are all desires but dust to the feet? I fear above all things the unforgiving love of Him who has dominion. But great love, great hope, these touch with immortal lips my phantom frailties. What day can be vain when I know within myself that I am kin to spirits who do not pass as smoke and flame?'

But because one can understand a man best from what reach he has or had, than from any or all of his poor fallings away, I learned more from a vellum-bound MS. book, written also on vellum, as though he held it as his particular and most intimate utterance, which he gave me the day before he died. For there are many among us who become transparent through the light of their imagination: who, when they mould images of thought and dream, reveal their true selves with an insight that is at once beautiful and terrible. My friend was of these: and I recall seldom, and with ever less heed, the morbid agonies and elations, the bitter perversities, the idle veering of shaken thought, to remember what he wrote, not openly of himself or his own apparent life and yet wholly and poignantly and convincingly of himself, and of one whom he loved, in *The Book of the Opal.*

He gave me also the rare and beautiful stone after which he had named his book. He told me that it possessed occult powers, but whether of itself, or in the making of its perfect beauty, he could not say; or simply because of its beauty, and because perfect beauty has an infinite radiation and can attract not only influences, but powers. It may well be so.

I read often in this *Book of the Opal.* It is, to me, as the sea is, or the wind: for, like the unseen and homeless creature which in the beginning God breathed between the lips of Heat and Cold, it is full of unbidden meanings and has sighs and laughters: and, like the sea, it has limits and shallows, but holds the stars, and has depths where light is dim and only the still, breathless soul listens; and has a sudden voice that is old as day and night, and is fed with dews and rains, and is salt and bitter.

It was not his will that it should be given to others. 'I would like three to read it,' he said: 'then, in time, it will be moonlight in many minds, and, through the few, thousands will know all in it that has deep meaning for any but myself. For now I am a husbandman who knows he shall not reap what he has sown, but is content if even one seed only sink and rise. ~~I see a forest of souls staring at the stars which are the fruit of the tree that shall grow from that single seed.~~'

This that he desired may or may not be: for there is another Husbandman who garners in His own way and at His own time. ~~But the seed has been sown: and three~~ have read *The Book of the Opal*.

. . . .

When I reached him I saw in his face the shadow ~~of that ill which none may gainsay~~. He was on a sofa which had been drawn close to the window. The house was in a poor and unfrequented part, but the windows looked across the Laguna Morte, and from the roof-garden one might see at sundown the spires of Padua, like white gossamer caught in that vast thicket of flame and delicate rose which was the West.

It was at this hour, at a sundown such as this, that I saw him. Already the sweat of death was on his brow, though he lived, as in a tremulous, uncertain balance of light and shadow, for seven days.

His mind dwelled almost wholly upon ~~ancient~~ things: ~~old~~ mysteries, old myths, gods, and ~~demoniacal powers~~, dreams, and the ~~august~~ revelation of eternal beauty.

One afternoon he gave me four small objects, of which three were made of ivory and gold, and the fourth was a stone or rounded of basalt double-sphered with gold.

I asked him what meaning they had, for I knew he gave them with meaning

'Do you not know?' he said. One was the small image of a sword, the other of a spear, the third of a cup.

Then I knew that he had given me the symbols of the four quarters of the earth, and of all the worlds of the universe: the stone for the North, the sword for the East, the spear for the South, and the cup for the West.

'Hold the sword against the light that I may see it,' he whispered; adding, after a while: 'I am tired of all thoughts of glory and wonder, of power, and of love that divides.'

The next day, at sundown, he asked me to hold the little gold and ivory spear against the light. 'I am tired,' he said, 'of all thoughts of dominion, of great kingdoms and empires that come and pass, of insatiable desires, and all that goes forth to smite and to conquer.'

On the day that followed I held before his dimmed eyes the little gold and ivory cup, white as milk in the pale gold of a rain-clear windy set. 'I am tired,' he said, 'of all thoughts of dreams that outlive the grave, and of fearless eyes looking at the stars, and of old heroisms, and mystery, and the beauty of all beauty.'

It was on the next day he died. At noon his faint breath bade me lift the dark stone of basalt, though he could not see that which I held before his eyes. I saw the shadow in his closed eyelids become tremulous and pale blue, like faint, wind-shaken smoke.

Among the impersonal episodic of The Book of the Opal I found diffuse and crude material, often nous with living thought — the thought of timeless imagination or which an oldtime romance of worlds has been woven: two world one as the other remote from us in though each in degree to be recove if neither till after a deeper 'sea-ch than any the modern world has known. Though the soul is the still water in which each of us may discern this 'sea-change'; Art, is the symbolic language of the alone, now, the common mirror which all may look. And, Art, must remember, is the recovery of a bewildered tra-o the tradition of Beauty and of and of Youth, that, like the a3

SD - #0124 - 300822 - C0 - 229/152/11 - PB - 9781330621776 - Gloss Lamination